OUTDOOR LIFE
THE SPORTSMAN

This Happened to Me!

AMAZING TRUE-LIFE EXPERIENCES FROM
THE READERS OF *Outdoor Life*

CREATIVE
PUBLISHING
international

MINNETONKA, MINNESOTA

Creative Publishing international, Inc.
5900 Green Oak Drive
Minnetonka, MN 55343
1-800-328-3895

Chairman: Iain Macfarlane
President/CEO: David D. Murphy
Vice President/Retail Sales & Marketing: James Knapp
Creative Director: Lisa Rosenthal

THIS HAPPENED TO ME!
Executive Editor, Outdoor Group: Don Oster
Project Leader and Article Editor : David L. Tieszen
Managing Editor: Jill Anderson
Associate Creative Director: Brad Springer
Senior Art Director: Dave Schelitzche
Assisting Art Director: Joe Fahey
Photo Researcher: Angie Hartwell
Mac Designer: Laurie Kristensen
Production Services Manager: Kim Gerber
Photographer: Tate Carlson

Contributing Illustrators: Dennis Budgen: cover: bottom right; pp. 3 bottom left,
220-223. Ken Laager: cover: top left, back cover; pp. 3 bottom right, 178, 179, 181-219.

Printed on American paper by: R. R. Donnelley & Sons Co.

10   9   8   7   6   5   4   3   2   1

Library of Congress Cataloging-in-Publication Data

This happened to me.
    p.   cm.
    ISBN 0-86573-107-1 (soft cover)
    1. Outdoor life--United States Comic books, strips, etc.
2. American wit and humor, Pictorial. I. Creative Publishing
International. II. Outdoor life (Denver, Colo.)
PN6728.T645 1999
741.5'973--dc21   99-27765

Outdoor Life is a Registered Trademark of Times Mirror Magazines, Inc.,
used under license by Creative Publishing international, Inc.

Table of Contents

Introduction

Even before I had the patience to read any of the features, I can recall scouring Dad's stacks of OUTDOOR LIFE in search of "the cartoon." Thumbing directly to "This Happened to Me," I'd relive the harrowing close call, then just as quickly toss the magazine aside and reach for the next issue. To an eight-year-old who had the run of seemingly endless woods around our cabin in northern Michigan, this was heady stuff. Real stuff, in fact. When the pines grew scary at dusk, it wasn't difficult to imagine those things happening to me: deadfalls became menacing bears, and squirrels' nests enormous rabid raccoons waiting in ambush overhead ... which I'd slay with my Swiss Army knife just as the snarling beast was upon me.

Those things never did happen to me. They almost never happen to any of us. But they could, which partly explains why "This Happened to Me" is so popular—vicarious triumphs usually are. For certain, they've always been popular with OUTDOOR LIFE's readership. Early issues of the magazine are peppered with gruesome dispatches from the frontier, of camp-marauding bears, devil cats and spectacularly lethal snowstorms. But in 1940, the magazine began telling some of these tales through an unexpected medium.

EVOLUTION OF "THIS HAPPENED TO ME"

'40s • "This Happened to Me" makes its debut in OUTDOOR LIFE, featuring the drawings of Frank Hubbard— as it will for the next 20 years.

'50s • The first major design change, as panel borders are tossed and a splash of color appears.
•A seamless segue, as Carl Pfeufer becomes only the second illustrator of THTM.

AS I EXPECTED, HE SUBMERGED AS I CAME UP—BUT NOT DEEPLY ENOUGH!

3

'60s • New artist Sam Glanzman brings an exciting stop-action style to the feature.

"Have you seen our new feature?" editor Raymond Brown wrote in the June issue that year. "The picture story is the first in a series that tell of actual, true-life experiences in the outdoors. If any incident, whether thrilling or humorous, of your hunting or fishing can be treated in this way, send us a word description of it."

The debut installment established the "This Happened to Me" formula. As cartoons go, it was no Funky Winkerbean; it was more like Mark Trail meets Ripley's Believe It or Not. Frothy-mouthed furbearers, toothy marine creatures and even Nature itself were portrayed as impending deliverers of death, and the sportsman as the generally innocent victim of their fury. Even when, as Brown wrote in his introduction, the strip presented the "lighter side of the outdoor experience," one thing was clear—some forces are beyond our control, especially in the wild.

The concept was an instant success, and it continues to be. In reader surveys, "This Happened to Me" is almost always the most-read feature. To the hopelessly analytical, the reason for its success might be elusive. What could be more predictable? The good guy (even when he's inept or stupid) always wins in the last panel.

There must be more. Perhaps the feature's secret is that it is quickly digested. Perhaps it's because the cartoon format holds promise of nonstop entertainment—a 20-second roller-coaster ride, so to speak.

But maybe it's as simple as an eight-year-old's reaction, which, not incidentally, was the first thing I thought of when just last fall I cut a fresh grizzly track two hours up a mountain: This is real stuff. This could happen to me.

Ed Scheff, Executive Editor, Outdoor Life

'70s

• After the strip takes a mysterious two-year hiatus, Richard Amundsen assumes control, and THTM finds a new home on the back page.

• A new spin on the formula, as several adventure tales are told in photographs.

• Following Amundsen, Gil Cohen takes over the feature for a brief one-year run as illustrator.

The youngster ran to his beached dinghy, and with help from his seven-hp outboard, managed to motor out to rescue us from our life and death predicament.

'80s

• Ken Laager provides a welcome new look and begins a 15-year stint as THTM illustrator.

'90s

• Finally! The feature earns a measure of respect as luxurious four-color arrives on the page.

• Dennis Budgen picks up the torch in the '90s and illustrates the column through July 1999. In August of 1999, Ken Laager returns as illustrator.

Dragged by a Runaway

In my youth I lived on the western plains of Nebraska.

One March day my father and uncle went duck hunting, losing the last few birds in the long grass, just before calling it a day.

Next morning I asked if I might take old Jack and get the duck feathers for my hope chest...

I'LL HAVE TO GO GET THE SADDLE AT UNCLE'S FIRST

THE COYOTES BEAT ME TO IT! — WE MAY AS WELL GO BACK, JACK

STEADY, JACK — STEADY, BOY

Horse

By Mrs. T. E. Adams, Pagosa Springs, Colorado

Double Peril on a Pig

Hunt

By Jorge Garay Silva, Mexico City, Mexico

Double Danger in the

THE GIANT BOAR LAY QUIVERING ON THE GROUND, KILLED WITH ONE SHOT FROM MY .45 — A LUCKY HIT — AND THE NEW GUINEA JUNGLE WAS LOUD WITH THE PROTESTS OF COCKATOOS. NOW THE SQUADRON WOULD HAVE FRESH MEAT, AND FOR THE FIRST TIME IN SEVERAL WEEKS . . .

IT WAS ONLY A MILE TO CAMP. THE EASIEST WAY WAS TO SWIM HIM THERE — AND RETURN FOR MY UNIFORM LATER

HALFWAY TO CAMP

PIG MUST BE SNAGGED ON SOMETHING

Jungle

By Captain David F. Harbour, Army Air Forces

The Day I Put My Foot

HUNTING DEER IN THE WATERSMEET DISTRICT OF NORTHERN MICHIGAN, A FEW MILES NORTH OF THE WISCONSIN LINE, I ENTERED A THICK TANGLE OF WINDFALLEN TREES • • •

—PUSHING MY GUN ON AHEAD OF ME UNDER A BIG TREE, I CLIMBED OVER—

GUN

in It

By Harold Damoth, Wayland, Michigan

One Cast I'll Never

Forget

By Herbert Wills, Morgantown, West Virginia

The Day I Lost My Grip

By Thomas H. Ramey, Gate City, Virginia

Danger in a Dory

By Don Holm, Oakland, California

THE BARGE SWUNG AROUND IN THE WIND, WITH THE TOW HAWSER UNDER OUR BOAT. AS THE TUG BACKED UP, THE HAWSER BECAME TAUT, AND LIFTED US OUT OF THE WATER

NEXT MORNING

SORRY ABOUT YOUR DORY, BOYS

WE'LL SETTLE FOR JUST BEING HERE

A Call for Help in

GUILLERMO, MY INDIAN GUIDE, AND I WERE FLOATING DOWN THE CHU-CANAQUI RIVER, DARIEN PROVINCE, REPUBLIC OF PANAMA, IN OUR CANOE ON OUR WAY OUT FOR SUPPLIES.

Panama

By William C. Greene, Curundu, Canal Zone

Rocky Mountain

WE WERE ON OUR WAY TO AVALANCHE LAKE IN THE FLATHEAD NATIONAL FOREST IN MONTANA, THE SUPERINTENDENT AND I, TO SEE IF A BRIDGE COULD BE BUILT ACROSS THE CREEK ECONOMICALLY.
I ALWAYS HAD A CRAZE FOR A PET ANIMAL AROUND THE STATION.
AT THE FOOT OF THE LAKE. .

HEY! LOOK AT THE GOATS CROSSING THE LAKE!

HERE'S MY CHANCE TO TAKE HOME A PET—WATCH MY SMOKE!

PICK A LITTLE ONE, FRANK!

Dynamite

By Frank Liebig, Forest Ranger

Rough Stuff in the

Night

By J. A. Schlegel, Montesano, Washington

Ungrateful Elk

I WORK ON THE NATIONAL ELK REFUGE AT JACKSON, WYOMING IN WINTER WHEN WE ARE FEEDING THE ELK, I USE A SHORT CUT SNOW ROAD ACROSS THE FROZEN SWAMP TO GET TO THE HAY SHEDS.
ALONG THE ROUTE ARE A NUMBER OF BOGS, DANGEROUS BECAUSE THEY NEVER FREEZE, THEIR DECEPTIVE COVERING OF SNOW MAKING CONCEALED ELK TRAPS OF THEM.
ON MY WAY TO WORK ONE MORNING —

NOW YOU'RE O.K., OLD GIRL!

By E. H. Pratt, Jackson, Wyoming

Panther's Day at Home

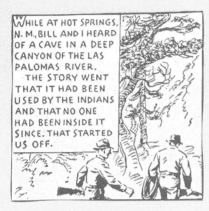

Hard Way to Get a

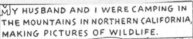

Photo

By Ada M. Morgan, Lafayette, California

Bulldozer Nightmare

When I was with the U.S. Forest Service, Seavey and I had been fighting a fire all day. We were about three jumps ahead of exhaustion. Late that night —

RELIEF AT LAST, GEORGE!

IT'S NOT GOING TO TAKE ME LONG TO FIND A PLACE TO FLOP!

ME NEITHER!

SLEEP TIGHT

'NIGHT BOYS

G'NIGHT

A BULLDOZER IS ORDERED BACK TO THE FIRE LINE —

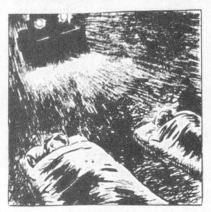

By George R. Stewart, Hollywood, California

A Rough Playmate

FISHING FROM A BOAT IS VERY GOOD ON THE NORTH FORK OF THE SNAKE RIVER, IDAHO. WE USUALLY HAULED OUR BOAT UPSTREAM, THEN ONE OF US WOULD DRIVE PART WAY BACK AND FISH WHILE HE WAITED FOR THE OTHERS. THAT DAY MY TURN CAME FIRST...

FIRST STOP

By William H. Dahlstrom, Idaho Falls, Idaho

Lion on the Lone

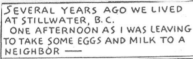

By *Mrs. Emma Pew, Port Kells, British Columbia*

SOME FOLKS SAY A COUGAR WILL NOT ATTACK A HUMAN, BUT DON'T YOU BELIEVE IT! THIS ONE WAS CAUGHT A FEW DAYS LATER

This Buck Was Well-

Concealed

By Harlan G. Barrett, N. Swanzey, New Hampshire

The Day I Played

ON LOCATION IN YELLOWSTONE PARK, A FILM COMPANY WAS SHOOTING A BUFFALO STAMPEDE. DAD AND I, DRESSED AS INDIANS, WERE TO RIDE IN IT.

WE START THE BUFFALOES TOWARD THE BLUFF ON WHICH THE CAMERAS ARE LOCATED.

Indian

By William T. Adams, Los Angeles, California

Free Ride

SITTING AROUND OUR CAMPFIRE AT LONG LAKE, CANADA, WE SAW, ON A SANDSPIT ACROSS A LITTLE BAY, A LARGE ANIMAL, INDISTINCT IN THE GATHERING DARKNESS.

HE'S BLOCKED OFF THIS WAY, ANYHOW!

By Major Carlos C. Alden Jr., Fort Benning, Georgia

No Rattle for Baby

WE LIVED IN THE WEST WHEN OUR OLDEST BOY WAS A BABY BARELY ABLE TO CRAWL. ONE DAY WHILE MY HUSBAND WAS AWAY ON A HUNTING TRIP IN THE MOUNTAINS · · · ·

FINISHING HANGING MY WASH, I PICKED UP THE BASKET AND AN EXTRA LENGTH OF CLOTHESLINE AND STARTED BACK INTO THE HOUSE

By Mrs. John Springer, Caddo, Oklahoma

Right Call — Wrong

Answer

By Robert L. Pigg, Kansas City, Missouri

Slinging the Bull

By John Howard, Bennington, Vermont

Fishline Ferry

I WENT FISHING IN JANUARY ON PLATTS-BURG BAY, AT THE NORTHERN END OF LAKE CHAMPLAIN, N.Y. REMEMBERING THE HABIT OF PERCH OF FOLLOWING THE EDGE OF ICE, I CUT A HOLE ABOUT 40 FT. FROM OPEN WATER, AND WAS DOING FINE UNTIL—

I LOOKED UP TO SEE THAT THE ICE I WAS ON HAD BROKEN AWAY FROM THE REST

IT'S TOO FAR TO JUMP!.

CUPPY! —CATCH!

By Glenn D. Clark, Plattsburgh, New York

Hard Way Out

WITH MY FRIEND DAVID PORTER, I WAS HUNTING FOXES AROUND LAKE POYGAN IN WISCONSIN. I WAS IN MY OLD SEDAN WITH THE TWO DOGS CROSSING ON THE ICE, AND DAVE WAS HALF A MILE AWAY ACROSS THE LAKE WHEN ....

By Henry Langenberg, Kimberly, Wisconsin

Photo Finish

By Thomas H. Nicoll, Champagne, Illinois

A Deer Can Get You

Down

By Ernest E. Dill, Portland, Oregon

Race on the Rangeland

HEADING HOME FROM A RABBIT HUNT IN A SPREAD OF CATTLE RANGELAND NEAR NIGHTINGALE, ALBERTA, I WASN'T FAR FROM A HERD OF COWS AND CALVES WHEN I NOTICED A STIR IN A NEAR-BY THICKET.

THE CATTLE, EXCITED BY THE COYOTE AND MY GUNSHOT, PAWING AND BELLOWING, SWUNG AROUND, FACING ME MENACINGLY.

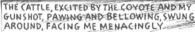

By Eddie Olnyuk, Nightingale, Alberta

Honeymoon Hazard

ON OUR HONEYMOON MY BRIDE AND I WERE HEADED FOR MY CABIN ON MANITOULIN ISLAND, ONTARIO

SHE CAME DOWN WITH A BAD CASE OF INFLUENZA ON THE WAY, AND WAS STILL VERY WEAK SIX DAYS LATER, OUR FOOD RUNNING LOW, I HAD TO GO FOR MORE – A 22-MILE TRIP

KEEP THE DOOR LOCKED FROM THE INSIDE

WHAT'S THAT NOISE?

HELP! HELP!

By Lee D. Beatty, Toronto, Ontario

Rough Playmates

By Albert Keller, San Francisco, California

Wild Horsepower

By Bud Odom, Chico, California

One for the Grab Bag

EIGHT MILES BACK FROM MILEPOST 804 ON THE ALASKA HIGHWAY IS NISUTLIN BAY, AN ARM OF LAKE TES-LIN, WHERE WE WERE DUCK HUNTING. A LONE MALLARD CAME SAILING IN.

FETCH IT, MIKE!

By G. R. Bidlake, Whitehorse, Yukon Territory

One of Us Had to Die

By *Homer L. Troutman, Concord, North Carolina*

THE DEER LEFT ME FOR DEAD

—BUT WHEN I STRUGGLED TO SHORE

SOMEHOW I WAS ABLE TO HOLD HIS HEAD UNDER WATER UNTIL HE DROWNED

HALF AN HOUR LATER I WAS FOUND, CARRIED HOME, AND RUSHED TO THE HOSPITAL

A Guide's "Day Off"

FOR 20 YEARS I HAVE BEEN A TRAPPER AND BIG-GAME GUIDE. ONE SUNDAY WE WERE SITTING OVER A LATE BREAKFAST IN OUR CABIN OVERLOOKING LAKE SHUSWAP IN BRITISH COLUMBIA · · ·

By Glory Temple, Sicamous, British Columbia

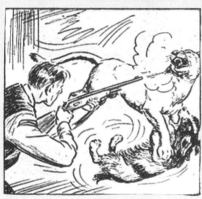

I HAD TO PRY THE COUGAR'S LEGS APART TO FREE MY DOG

WHEN I SKINNED OUT THE BIG CAT, I FOUND HIM AS BADLY CHEWED UP AS GEORGE WAS

Quick-Freeze Venison

We were hunting deer (doe season only) in Wisconsin. Nearing Windpudding Lake, we saw a buck crossing the ice. He broke through and couldn't get out. So, taking a rope and pushing an old boat, to spread our weight, we went to the rescue . . .

1

2

3

4

5

6

By Russell F. Haubner, McNaughton, Wisconsin

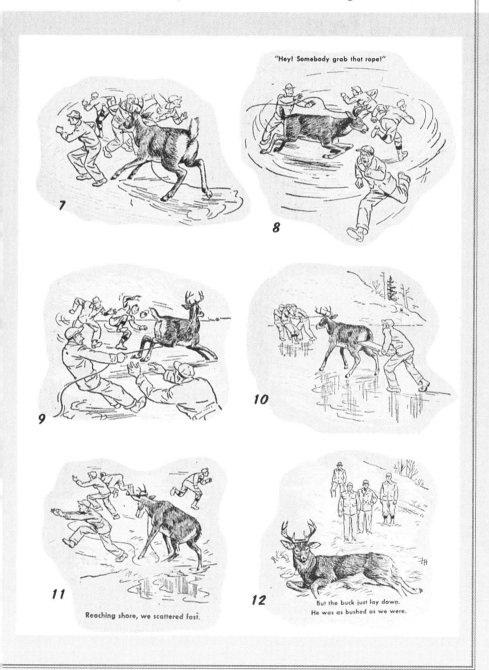

Dead Weight Saves the Day

By L. H. Fowler, Represa, California

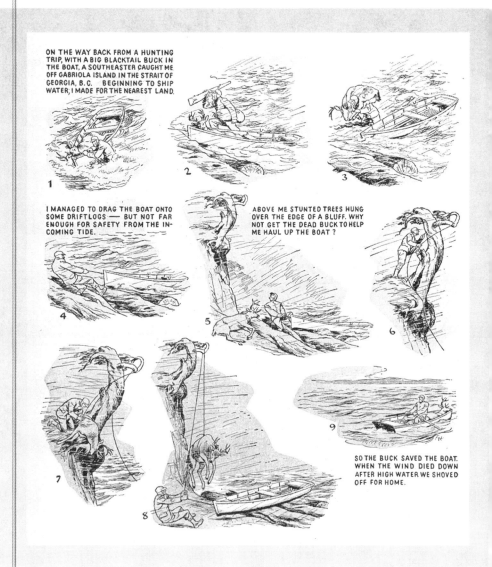

1. ON THE WAY BACK FROM A HUNTING TRIP, WITH A BIG BLACKTAIL BUCK IN THE BOAT, A SOUTHEASTER CAUGHT ME OFF GABRIOLA ISLAND IN THE STRAIT OF GEORGIA, B.C. BEGINNING TO SHIP WATER, I MADE FOR THE NEAREST LAND.

4. I MANAGED TO DRAG THE BOAT ONTO SOME DRIFTLOGS — BUT NOT FAR ENOUGH FOR SAFETY FROM THE INCOMING TIDE.

5. ABOVE ME STUNTED TREES HUNG OVER THE EDGE OF A BLUFF. WHY NOT GET THE DEAD BUCK TO HELP ME HAUL UP THE BOAT?

9. SO THE BUCK SAVED THE BOAT. WHEN THE WIND DIED DOWN AFTER HIGH WATER WE SHOVED OFF FOR HOME.

A Bear to Spare

By Clarence McLemore, Maryville, Tennessee

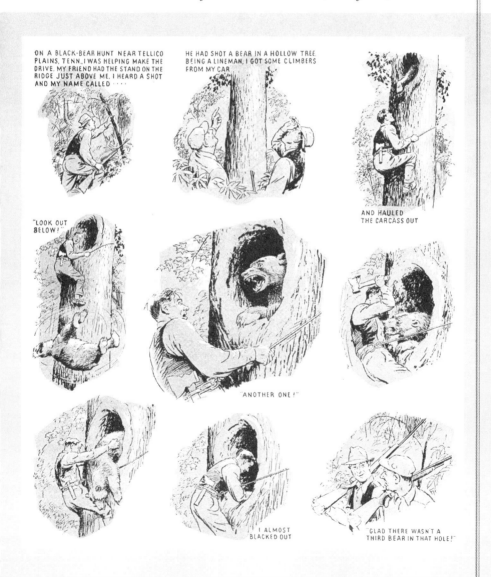

ON A BLACK-BEAR HUNT NEAR TELLICO PLAINS, TENN., I WAS HELPING MAKE THE DRIVE. MY FRIEND HAD THE STAND ON THE RIDGE JUST ABOVE ME. I HEARD A SHOT AND MY NAME CALLED · · · ·

HE HAD SHOT A BEAR IN A HOLLOW TREE. BEING A LINEMAN, I GOT SOME CLIMBERS FROM MY CAR

AND HAULED THE CARCASS OUT

"LOOK OUT BELOW!"

"ANOTHER ONE!"

I ALMOST BLACKED OUT

"GLAD THERE WASN'T A THIRD BEAR IN THAT HOLE!"

The Thing in the Tunnel

By Russell F. Haubner, McNaughton, Wisconsin

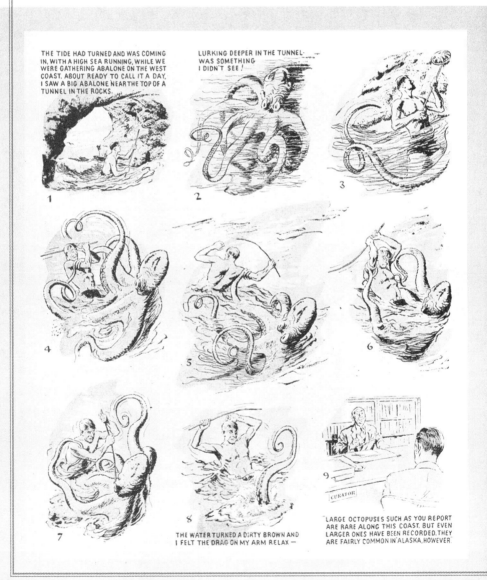

THE TIDE HAD TURNED AND WAS COMING IN, WITH A HIGH SEA RUNNING, WHILE WE WERE GATHERING ABALONE ON THE WEST COAST. ABOUT READY TO CALL IT A DAY, I SAW A BIG ABALONE NEAR THE TOP OF A TUNNEL IN THE ROCKS.

LURKING DEEPER IN THE TUNNEL WAS SOMETHING I DIDN'T SEE!

THE WATER TURNED A DIRTY BROWN AND I FELT THE DRAG ON MY ARM RELAX —

"LARGE OCTOPUSES SUCH AS YOU REPORT ARE RARE ALONG THIS COAST, BUT EVEN LARGER ONES HAVE BEEN RECORDED. THEY ARE FAIRLY COMMON IN ALASKA, HOWEVER"

CURATOR

Chased by a Gator

By Rossie Bushnell lll, De Land, Florida

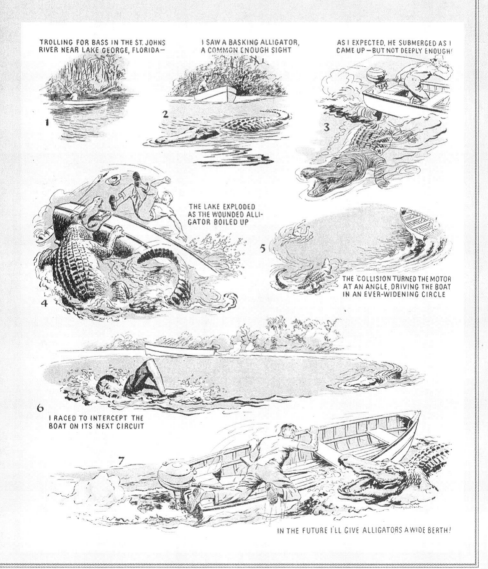

1. TROLLING FOR BASS IN THE ST. JOHNS RIVER NEAR LAKE GEORGE, FLORIDA—

2. I SAW A BASKING ALLIGATOR, A COMMON ENOUGH SIGHT

3. AS I EXPECTED, HE SUBMERGED AS I CAME UP—BUT NOT DEEPLY ENOUGH!

4. THE LAKE EXPLODED AS THE WOUNDED ALLIGATOR BOILED UP

5. THE COLLISION TURNED THE MOTOR AT AN ANGLE, DRIVING THE BOAT IN AN EVER-WIDENING CIRCLE

6. I RACED TO INTERCEPT THE BOAT ON ITS NEXT CIRCUIT

7. IN THE FUTURE I'LL GIVE ALLIGATORS A WIDE BERTH!

No Holds Barred

By Frank Orosco, Escondido, California

1. I WAS IRRIGATING MY AVOCADOS ON MY RANCH NEAR ESCONDIDO, CALIF. WHEN MY DOG ZIPPED PAST, CLOSELY TAILED BY....

3. THE WILDCAT LEFT THE DOG AND TURNED ON ME. I HAD DROPPED MY SHOVEL OUT OF REACH — MY FLASHLIGHT!

I WON THE BATTLE BUT IT COST ME MANY SCARS

Saved by a Razorback

By Robert R. Ozmer, Everglades, Florida

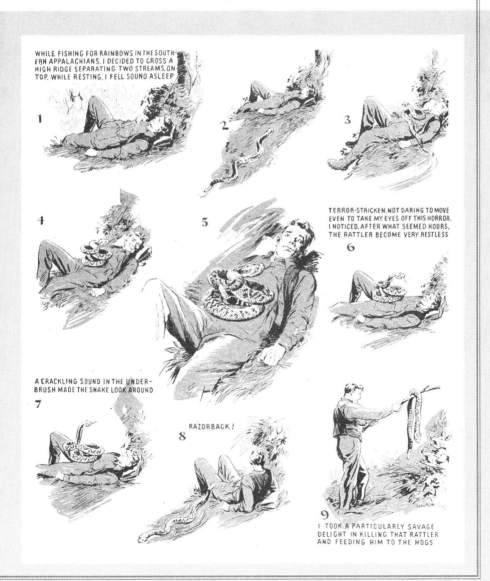

1 WHILE FISHING FOR RAINBOWS IN THE SOUTHERN APPALACHIANS, I DECIDED TO CROSS A HIGH RIDGE SEPARATING TWO STREAMS. ON TOP, WHILE RESTING, I FELL SOUND ASLEEP

2

3

4

5

6 TERROR-STRICKEN, NOT DARING TO MOVE EVEN TO TAKE MY EYES OFF THIS HORROR, I NOTICED, AFTER WHAT SEEMED HOURS, THE RATTLER BECOME VERY RESTLESS

7 A CRACKLING SOUND IN THE UNDERBRUSH MADE THE SNAKE LOOK AROUND

8 RAZORBACK!

9 I TOOK A PARTICULARLY SAVAGE DELIGHT IN KILLING THAT RATTLER AND FEEDING HIM TO THE HOGS

Heron-Pecked

By H. K. McClernon, Reading, Vermont

1. WHILE HUNTING IN CONNECTICUT, I CAME UPON A LARGE BLUE HERON CAUGHT IN A MUSKRAT TRAP. I DECIDED TO RESCUE HIM AND SEE IF HE WAS BADLY INJURED

2.

3. FORCING THE BIRD'S HEAD UNDER HIS WING, I BENT OVER TO REPLACE THE TRAP

4.

5. WITH A LIGHTNING THRUST THE HERON STRUCK AT MY LEFT EYE. I LET GO, BUT HE FOUGHT ON, NOT REALIZING HE WAS FREE

6.

7.

8. I FINALLY STOPPED THE BLEEDING WITH COLD COMPRESSES

9. ONLY MY FAST DUCKING SAVED ME. HAD THE BIRD HIT MY EYE, IT COULD HAVE KILLED ME, MY DOCTOR SAID.

Cold Wave Coming

By Allan E. Hennessy, Seward, Alaska

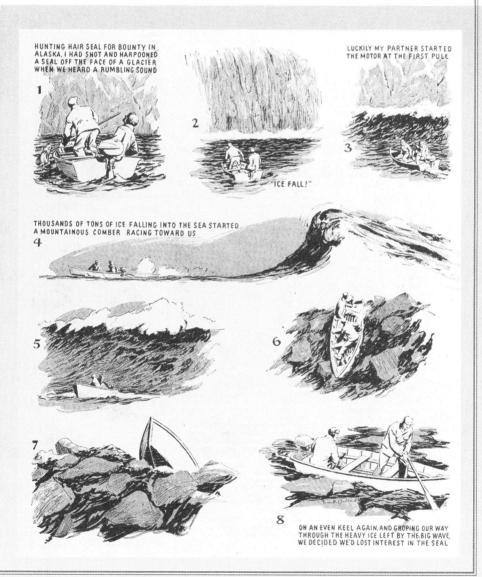

1. HUNTING HAIR SEAL FOR BOUNTY IN ALASKA, I HAD SHOT AND HARPOONED A SEAL OFF THE FACE OF A GLACIER WHEN WE HEARD A RUMBLING SOUND

2. "ICE FALL!"

3. LUCKILY MY PARTNER STARTED THE MOTOR AT THE FIRST PULL

4. THOUSANDS OF TONS OF ICE FALLING INTO THE SEA STARTED A MOUNTAINOUS COMBER RACING TOWARD US

8. ON AN EVEN KEEL AGAIN, AND GROPING OUR WAY THROUGH THE HEAVY ICE LEFT BY THE BIG WAVE, WE DECIDED WE'D LOST INTEREST IN THE SEAL

Politeness Pays

By George Dillon, Denver, Colorado

1. WHILE WORKING IN ALASKA ONE SUMMER, MY FRIEND BILL AND I WERE FISHING FOR STEELHEADS. IN LANDING A LARGE ONE I BROKE THE TIP OF MY ROD AND SAT DOWN TO FIX IT. THE FISH, TOO BIG FOR MY CREEL, LAY BESIDE ME...

3. A HUGE BROWNIE!

4. I BACKED RIGHT OUT OF THOSE BUSHES—POLITELY—SORT OF

5. —AND KEPT RIGHT ON BACKING...

6. —BACKING...

7. —BACKING!

9. BILL GOT ME TO SHORE, BUT IT WASN'T UNTIL WE HAD WRUNG OURSELVES OUT THAT I COULD SEE THE HUMOROUS SIDE OF WHAT HAD HAPPENED TO ME.

The Black Cat

By Derek Horvath, Vancouver, British Columbia

A BLACK LEOPARD HAD BEEN KILLING STOCK ON OUR SOUTH AFRICAN FARM. WHILE HUNTING STRAYS, MY PARTNER CARL AND I FOUND THE CARCASS OF A FRESHLY KILLED YEARLING. WE STARTED AFTER THE CAT, WITH ONLY AN ANCIENT 25/40 SINGLE-SHOT RIFLE BETWEEN US.

1

2

3

BEFORE CARL COULD GET TO HIS FEET THE LEOPARD WAS UPON HIM

4

MY BULLET ONLY GRAZED THE CAT'S HEAD

5

6

I FELL HEAVILY UPON THE GUN

7

BUT CARL WRENCHED IT FREE AND RELOADED IN THE NICK OF TIME

8

9

SUPPORTING EACH OTHER, WE STUMBLED HOMEWARD UNTIL WE MET A SEARCH PAR-TY THAT HAD BEEN ORGANIZED WHEN OUR HORSES RETURNED RIDERLESS.

Bounty Mutiny

By Harold Davidson, Vermillion, South Dakota

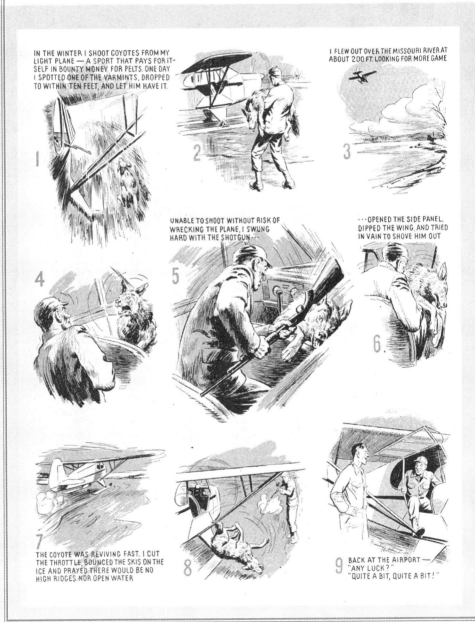

1. IN THE WINTER I SHOOT COYOTES FROM MY LIGHT PLANE — A SPORT THAT PAYS FOR ITSELF IN BOUNTY MONEY, FOR PELTS. ONE DAY I SPOTTED ONE OF THE VARMINTS, DROPPED TO WITHIN TEN FEET, AND LET HIM HAVE IT.

3. I FLEW OUT OVER THE MISSOURI RIVER AT ABOUT 200 FT. LOOKING FOR MORE GAME

5. UNABLE TO SHOOT WITHOUT RISK OF WRECKING THE PLANE, I SWUNG HARD WITH THE SHOTGUN···

6. ···OPENED THE SIDE PANEL, DIPPED THE WING, AND TRIED IN VAIN TO SHOVE HIM OUT

7. THE COYOTE WAS REVIVING FAST. I CUT THE THROTTLE, BOUNCED THE SKIS ON THE ICE AND PRAYED THERE WOULD BE NO HIGH RIDGES NOR OPEN WATER

9. BACK AT THE AIRPORT — "ANY LUCK?" "QUITE A BIT, QUITE A BIT!"

Booby-Trapped

By Walker D. Wallace, Fairhope, Alabama

1. WHEN I WAS TRAPPING THE MARSHES NEAR MOBILE, ALA., SOME OF MY BEST MUSKRAT SETS WERE NEAR A BEAR TRAIL THAT RAN THROUGH A TANGLE OF BRIARS. BEARS USED THIS TUNNEL BY NIGHT...

2. AND I TRAVELED IT BY DAY IN RUNNING MY TRAPS. ONE MORNING I HAD AN ODD PREMONITION.

3. I CREPT AHEAD CAUTIOUSLY—

4. —PROBING WITH A FORKED STICK SUCH AS MOST MARSHLAND TRAPPERS CARRY....

7. I'D BEEN CATAPULTED FROM THE JAW OF A HUGE BEAR TRAP!

8. I REMOVED THE TRAP FROM ITS DRAG AND SUNK IT IN THE MARSH

9. I HAD TROUBLE FINDING OUT WHO HAD SET THE ILLEGAL TRAP, BUT WHEN I DID I THREW A SCARE INTO HIM THAT HE WON'T FORGET.

Last Cartridge

By Paul Lehrer, Kijabe, Kenya Colony, East Africa

1. TO SUPPLY MEAT FOR OUR MISSION STATION IN KENYA COLONY, EAST AFRICA, I USED TO HUNT ANTELOPE ON NEAR-BY MT. LONGONOT. ONE MORNING, AS I GLASSED THE SLOPES... CAPE BUFFALO!

2. "WHAT ABOUT BUFFALO STEAK INSTEAD OF VENISON TODAY?"

6. MY .30/06 RIFLE WAS FAR TOO LIGHT FOR SUCH GAME, AND I MERELY WOUNDED A BIG BUFFALO. NOW, TO MY HORROR, I FOUND I HAD ONLY ONE CARTRIDGE LEFT!

7. I SAT DOWN FOR A CAREFUL SHOT WITH MY LAST BULLET...

9. "IF I'D HAD ONE CARTRIDGE LESS, THE BULL WOULD BE THE TOP MAN!"

Clinch with a 'Cuda

By Edmond L. Fisher, Miami, Florida

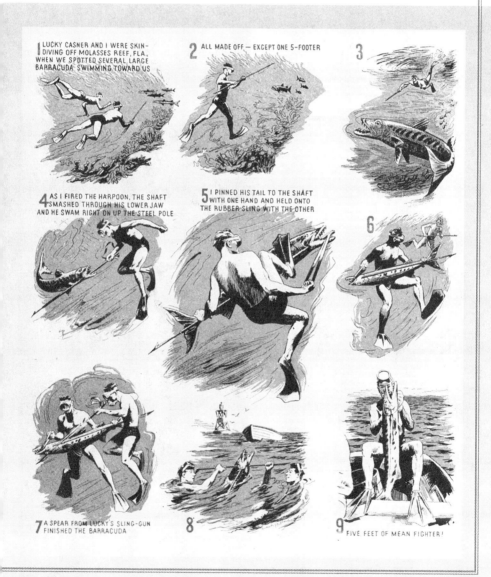

1 LUCKY CASNER AND I WERE SKIN-DIVING OFF MOLASSES REEF, FLA., WHEN WE SPOTTED SEVERAL LARGE BARRACUDA SWIMMING TOWARD US

2 ALL MADE OFF — EXCEPT ONE 5-FOOTER

3

4 AS I FIRED THE HARPOON, THE SHAFT SMASHED THROUGH HIS LOWER JAW AND HE SWAM RIGHT ON UP THE STEEL POLE

5 I PINNED HIS TAIL TO THE SHAFT WITH ONE HAND AND HELD ONTO THE RUBBER SLING WITH THE OTHER

6

7 A SPEAR FROM LUCKY'S SLING-GUN FINISHED THE BARRACUDA

8

9 FIVE FEET OF MEAN FIGHTER!

The Persuader

By Ted Shatto, Boyes Hot Spring, California

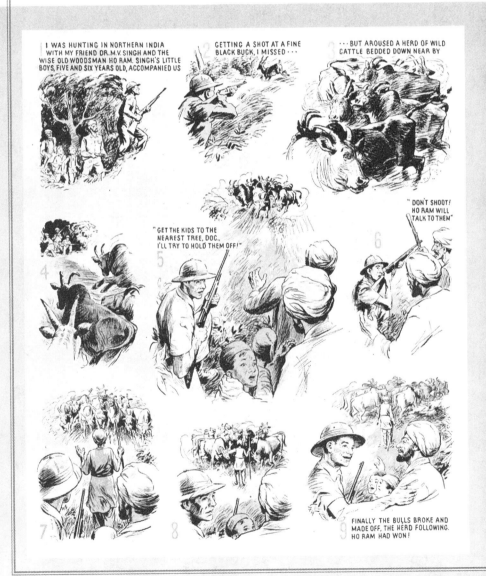

1 I WAS HUNTING IN NORTHERN INDIA WITH MY FRIEND DR. M.V. SINGH AND THE WISE OLD WOODSMAN HO RAM. SINGH'S LITTLE BOYS, FIVE AND SIX YEARS OLD, ACCOMPANIED US

2 GETTING A SHOT AT A FINE BLACK BUCK, I MISSED · · ·

3 · · · BUT AROUSED A HERD OF WILD CATTLE BEDDED DOWN NEAR BY

5 " GET THE KIDS TO THE NEAREST TREE, DOC., I'LL TRY TO HOLD THEM OFF!"

6 " DON'T SHOOT! HO RAM WILL TALK TO THEM"

9 FINALLY THE BULLS BROKE AND MADE OFF, THE HERD FOLLOWING. HO RAM HAD WON!

I Got Stung

By Harvey L. Guntzviller, Northville, Michigan

HUNTING ALONG THE FLATHEAD RIVER IN WESTERN MONTANA, WE WERE ON THE SPOTTED BEAR TRAIL WHEN THE LEAD HORSE STEPPED INTO A HORNETS' NEST

MY HORSE'S MISSTEP HAD BROKEN MY LEG. I WAS HELPLESS AND UNPROTECTED AGAINST THE RAGING SWARMS OF HORNETS!

SOMEONE THREW A COAT OVER ME...

WHICH ONLY MADE MATTERS WORSE, BY TRAPPING THE HORNETS INSIDE. I HAD TO KILL EVERY ONE OF THEM

HELP WAS SOON AT HAND. ONE OF THE PARTY, A SPOKANE DOCTOR, PUT AN EMERGENCY SPLINT ON MY LEG

I HAD TO RIDE SIX MILES TO THE FOREST SERVICE AIRFIELD. FROM THERE A PLANE TOOK ME TO A MISSOULA HOSPITAL.

Hog Wild

By Jean Laperous, Fairhope, Alabama

1. RUNNING A HUNDRED MUSKRAT TRAPS IN THE ALABAMA MARSHES BORDERING MOBILE BAY, I HAD JUST RESET A TRAP AT THE END OF THE LINE A HALF MILE FROM MY BOAT, WHEN A RUSTLE IN THE GRASS MADE ME LOOK UP. I KNEW ABOUT THE WILD HOGS THEREABOUTS, BUT WHAT I SAW FROZE MY BLOOD!

3. THE BOAR STRUCK WITH ALL THE SAVAGERY OF A CHARGING BULL, SLASHING MY LEFT LEG BADLY

7. MY LAST SHOT FINISHED HIM. I MADE A TOURNIQUET OUT OF MY SHIRTTAIL. WEAK FROM LOSS OF BLOOD, I HAD TO GET TO MY BOAT

9. AFTER DRYING OUT, I RAN THE BOAT TO THE CAUSEWAY AND CAUGHT A RIDE TO MOBILE, WHERE I WAS LAID UP FOR TWO WEEKS. I CARRIED MY GUN AND PLENTY OF AMMO FOR THE REST OF THE SEASON.

Playing Possum

By W. E. Hamm, Douglas, Georgia

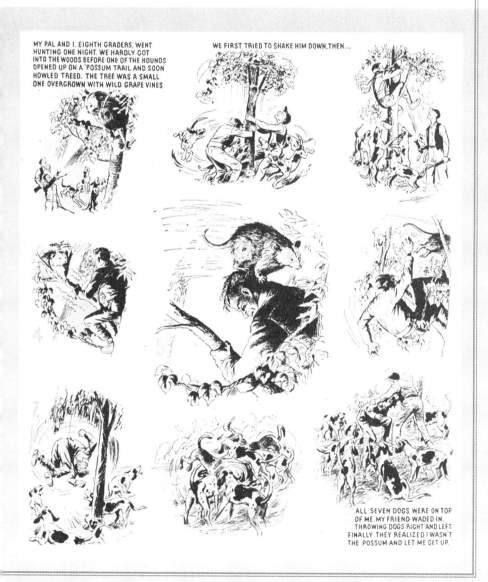

MY PAL AND I, EIGHTH GRADERS, WENT HUNTING ONE NIGHT. WE HARDLY GOT INTO THE WOODS BEFORE ONE OF THE HOUNDS OPENED UP ON A 'POSSUM TRAIL AND SOON HOWLED TREED. THE TREE WAS A SMALL ONE OVERGROWN WITH WILD GRAPE VINES

WE FIRST TRIED TO SHAKE HIM DOWN, THEN...

ALL SEVEN DOGS WERE ON TOP OF ME. MY FRIEND WADED IN, THROWING DOGS RIGHT AND LEFT. FINALLY THEY REALIZED I WASN'T THE POSSUM AND LET ME GET UP.

Unwanted Guest

By Tony Burmek, Milwaukee, Wisconsin

1. WHILE THE COUPLE I WAS GUIDING IN CANADA TOOK A WALK ALONG THE SHORE OF A LAKE, I FRIED FISH FOR SUPPER. I THOUGHT THEY WERE RETURNING WHEN I HEARD A NOISE BEHIND ME

2.

3. I TRIED TO FRIGHTEN HIM OFF, WAVING MY AX WILDLY · · ·

4. BUT THIS ONLY INFURIATED HIM. I SHOUTED TO MY GUESTS TO TAKE TO THE BOAT

5.

6. MISSING HIS HEAD, I STRUCK HIS RIGHT SHOULDER SOLIDLY. HE STAGGERED FOR A MOMENT · · ·

7. I SWUNG AGAIN, AIMING BETWEEN HIS EYES · · ·

8. THIS TIME MY AX HIT THE MARK

9. I STUMBLED FROM THE SPOT, EXHAUSTED, BUT A MIGHTY HAPPY INDIVIDUAL AND AN ETERNALLY GRATEFUL ONE.

Bad Noose

By Donald E. Spencer, Alexandria, Virginia

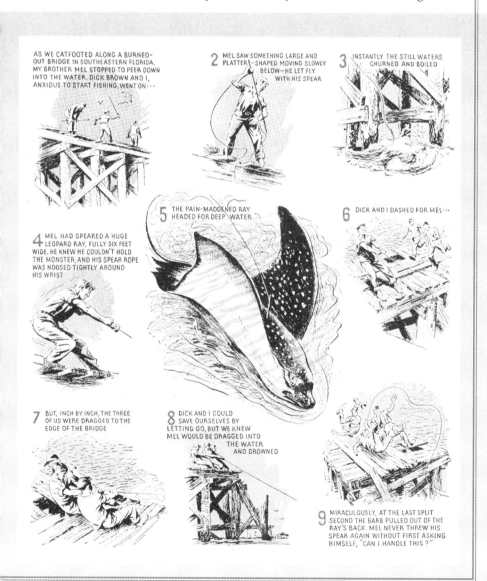

1. AS WE CATFOOTED ALONG A BURNED-OUT BRIDGE IN SOUTHEASTERN FLORIDA, MY BROTHER MEL STOPPED TO PEER DOWN INTO THE WATER. DICK BROWN AND I, ANXIOUS TO START FISHING, WENT ON...

2. MEL SAW SOMETHING LARGE AND PLATTER-SHAPED MOVING SLOWLY BELOW—HE LET FLY WITH HIS SPEAR

3. INSTANTLY THE STILL WATERS CHURNED AND BOILED

4. MEL HAD SPEARED A HUGE LEOPARD RAY, FULLY SIX FEET WIDE. HE KNEW HE COULDN'T HOLD THE MONSTER, AND HIS SPEAR ROPE WAS NOOSED TIGHTLY AROUND HIS WRIST

5. THE PAIN-MADDENED RAY HEADED FOR DEEP WATER

6. DICK AND I DASHED FOR MEL...

7. BUT, INCH BY INCH, THE THREE OF US WERE DRAGGED TO THE EDGE OF THE BRIDGE

8. DICK AND I COULD SAVE OURSELVES BY LETTING GO, BUT WE KNEW MEL WOULD BE DRAGGED INTO THE WATER AND DROWNED

9. MIRACULOUSLY, AT THE LAST SPLIT SECOND THE BARB PULLED OUT OF THE RAY'S BACK. MEL NEVER THREW HIS SPEAR AGAIN WITHOUT FIRST ASKING HIMSELF, "CAN I HANDLE THIS?"

No Weaseling

By Wayne Cowie, Calgary, Alberta

1. I WAS HUNTING PHEASANTS IN ALBERTA, CANADA. HEARING A RUSTLING NOISE IN THE UNDERBRUSH, I SLIPPED OFF THE SAFETY AND STOOD DEAD STILL···

2. WHEN A LARGE WEASEL RAN UP A FENCE POST···

3. AND HURTLED STRAIGHT AT MY THROAT!

4. WITH A YELL, I MANAGED TO FLING HIM OFF

5. HE CHARGED ME AGAIN. I SHOT FROM THE HIP — BUT MISSED!

6. HE CAME ON ONCE MORE, AND I TOOK CAREFUL AIM

7. THE SHOT DISEMBOWELED THE ANIMAL BUT DIDN'T KILL HIM

8. WITH A PIECE OF MY COAT SLEEVE IN HIS MOUTH, HE CRAWLED TOWARD ME, STILL FULL OF FIGHT, THEN DIED

9. WHY WOULD SUCH A SMALL ANIMAL ATTACK A MAN? I FIGURED HE MUST HAVE BEEN STARVED, DUE TO THE LATE HATCH OF PHEASANTS HAVING BEEN FROZEN TO DEATH.

Saved by a Trap

By Willie B. Hutcheson, Ridgely, Tennessee

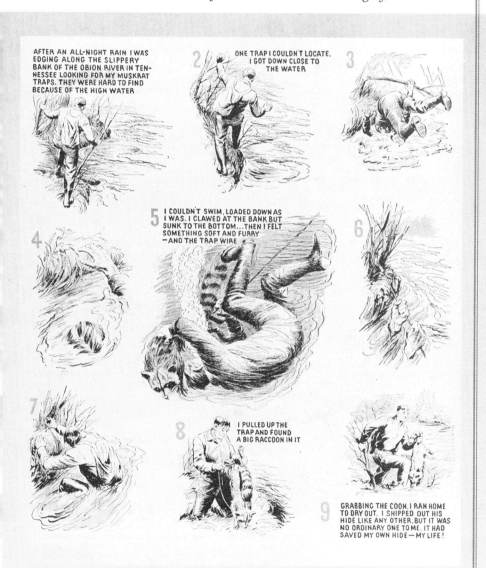

1. AFTER AN ALL-NIGHT RAIN I WAS EDGING ALONG THE SLIPPERY BANK OF THE OBION RIVER IN TENNESSEE LOOKING FOR MY MUSKRAT TRAPS. THEY WERE HARD TO FIND BECAUSE OF THE HIGH WATER

2. ONE TRAP I COULDN'T LOCATE. I GOT DOWN CLOSE TO THE WATER

5. I COULDN'T SWIM, LOADED DOWN AS I WAS. I CLAWED AT THE BANK BUT SUNK TO THE BOTTOM...THEN I FELT SOMETHING SOFT AND FURRY — AND THE TRAP WIRE

8. I PULLED UP THE TRAP AND FOUND A BIG RACCOON IN IT

9. GRABBING THE COON, I RAN HOME TO DRY OUT. I SHIPPED OUT HIS HIDE LIKE ANY OTHER, BUT IT WAS NO ORDINARY ONE TO ME. IT HAD SAVED MY OWN HIDE — MY LIFE !

Under a Cloud

By Lyman Hilliard, Atlanta, Georgia

Bass fishing at Clark Hill Lake, on the Georgia-South Carolina line, John and I were having fair luck. We'd noticed the unusual stillness. Later I was startled to see a wall of water rushing at us under a big black cloud.

It was apparent that the storm might catch us before we could make shore.

We ran the boat aground at top speed as the tornado hit us with full force.

Unable to stand up against the wind at first, we had to lie down flat.

Then I held the boat's painter as we dived for the shelter of a tree stump.

Broken branches and uprooted trees flew past, one narrowly missing us.

The tornado roared, pelting us with debris for what seemed an eternity.

We both say it was the closest call we've ever had in all our experience.

Who's Who?

By Joe R. Naccarato, Kellogg, Idaho

At dusk one summer day, while manning a fire tower in Idaho, I looked up and saw a great horned owl diving at me. I ducked flat onto the catwalk.

Missing me by inches, the owl flew off. I ran inside for my .22 pistol.

The bird came at me again, but I got off several shots that scared it away.

A week later, out cutting wood, I was attacked again. Again I scared it off.

Two weeks after that I was toting a water pack, when suddenly—Whammo!

A terrific jolt smashing against my back knocked me flat. It was the owl!!

Slashing with deadly talons and beak, it tore into my water pack and shirt.

Finally I turned over, shot it. Why did it attack? I still can't figure it out.

Snake in the Grass

By A. J. Guichet, New Orleans, Louisiana

Duck hunting in Louisiana, I was paddling up a canal when I saw a flock on a lagoon ahead. I eased my pirogue close to the bank, and picked up my gun.

Watching the ducks, I didn't notice a big cottonmouth on the bank not 2 ft. from me.

I fired my gun so close to the snake it scared him. He struck for my face.

Terrified, I hit the snake with the gun. It fell into the boat, then came for me.

Pinning him down, I accidentally fired the gun, blowing a hole in the pirogue.

I'd killed the snake, but by now I'd drifted far offshore and was sinking.

Plugs didn't work, so I hustled astern, my weight lifting the hole above water.

This is how I paddled the mile back to dry land. And was that water cold!

Epic Rescue

By Ralph Haynes, Cherokee, Kansas

While fishing in a Kansas coal-strip area with my brother-in-law and three-year-old boy one cold spring day, I started with my son across a high bank.

Suddenly the top of the bank sloughed off and my son tumbled 30 feet into icy water.

Luckily my plug hooked into his sweater, and I was able to hold him at the surface.

By brother-in-law jumped in, but the wall was too sheer for him even to hold onto.

I started down, then realized how foolish that would be, and quickly scrambled back.

Frantically I looked around, and saw a twist of barbed-wire fence in the weeds.

Tearing the wire loose, I threw it over the side and dragged them up to safety.

I took my son in my arms. That old wire, and my brother-in-law, had saved my world.

Killer Buffalo

By A. J. Smalley, St. George, Maine

On a Philippine timber survey, my guide and I were surrounded by wild buffaloes. Tomas climbed a vine as a buffalo charged, but it gave way.

The buffalo caught him on its horns and tossed him over its head into the jungle.

I shot the beast in the neck and it fell dead. Tomas lay unconscious not far away.

Then another one charged me and caught my rifle on its horns as I jumped aside.

While the animal shook off the rifle, I climbed a small tree and drew out my .45.

As the brute tried to butt down the tree, I shot it in the neck and both front legs.

I dropped to the ground, but it began to chase me. I threw my shirt over its head.

Luckily Tomas came to, hamstrung the buff with his bolo knife, and we finished it.

Our Cover Story

By L. J. Smith, Thompson Fall, Montana

Riding along a rugged Montana trail, my wife and I suddenly spotted a mother grizzly with three cubs. Foolishly, our dog tried chasing them.

In a rage, the huge sow made for us. I maneuvered desperately to let my wife get away first.

My horse panicked and almost threw me as the bear took a vicious swipe at him (see cover).

I finally got my horse turned and headed away, but the bear charged and tried to strike us again. I hesitated to use my six-shooter except as a last resort.

Rounding a bend, we stopped to collect our wits, but the bears came charging after us.

For a third time the sow tried to hit us, but we rode hard and got out of the area.

We took a beating from our bear-shy mounts when we returned later.

Rabid Fox

By Fred Gilliam, Athens, Texas

One winter day, accompanying me on my rounds as game warden, Wildlife Agent M. H. Boone missed a shot at a fox we thought appeared rabid.

It circled a vacant house, and came for us. I fired, missed. Then Boone got the shotgun.

We jumped into the car, but the fox was too close for us to use the gun. Twice it sprung to grab the barrel in its teeth.

The animal leaped at my window, then bounded on the hood. When it slipped off, we turned the car around to chase it.

Boone fired the shotgun, but the birdshot failed to drop the fox.

It kept on the road, and some 300 yards farther on we ran over it and killed it.

We heard later two men, bitten by a mad fox, were receiving rabies shots.

Beset by Dogs

By Gary Wehrle, Erie, Pennsylvania

Out hunting one day, I heard dogs barking and saw a deer coming my way. I thought he'd turn, but he knocked me against a tree.

Slightly dazed, I heard the dogs coming closer, and down hill I saw the mangiest pack of wild dogs I'd ever seen.

I had my gun set as they started by, but suddenly the lead dog saw me and stopped.

Fangs bared, the vicious beast leaped on me. My shot went wild.

Instantly, the whole snarling pack was at me, tearing and biting at my heavy hunting clothes.

I tried desperately to get away by rolling downhill, but they kept after me. I lay motionless as they ripped my clothing to shreds.

Suddenly they left and took after the deer again. I was badly scratched on hands and neck, but lucky to be alive.

Deadly Double

By V. M. Ocadiz R., Mexico

Javelina hunting on a Mexican ranch, I saw a bloody, trampled area. I followed the trail from it on foot.

I came upon a jaguar ripping a dead steer. As I raised my rifle to fire, a second jaguar appeared not 10 feet away.

I whirled, fired at it. The hammer clicked, but no shot rang out. The cat crouched for a spring.

Desperate, I grabbed my hat and flung it into the animal's face.

While he pawed it, I levered a cartridge into the chamber.

He leaped, and I fired a snapshot that hit his neck and killed him. I turned fast and fired at the other jaguar.

It fell dead. Why had my first shot failed? I'd neglected to load the chamber when I took the rifle from its scabbard!

Safe by a Nose

By Marvin Glenn, Douglas, Arizona

One morning on my ranch in Arizona's Chiricahua Mountains, my son, Warner, and I corralled a herd of wild mares for inspection.

We were busy checking them for bruises and worms and didn't notice that a stallion had come by for water.

I left the corral to get some medicine and suddenly saw the stallion nearby, watching me belligerently.

I've hunted mean mountain lions, but I've never seen a more vicious beast than this horse. Suddenly he charged me; I ran desperately.

Teeth bared and tail flying, the enraged horse gained on me. I thought I was a goner.

Just then my best lion hound leaped in to save me by nipping the horse's nose.

As the horse ran off, I patted my dog and thanked my stars he'd been there.

I Was in a Hole

By Earl Lail, Asheboro, North Carolina

While rabbit hunting in Cherryville, North Carolina, my four brothers, father, and myself came upon an abandoned farmhouse.

Behind it was a pile of brush and rotten lumber than looked as if it might hold a bunny. I went over to it.

The wood crumbled when I stepped on it, and down I plunged into a deserted well.

I plummeted 60 feet, and then hit the frigid water.

My brothers heard my yells, and ran for help. Meanwhile, I braced my feet and back against the well's slimy sides.

About a mile off, my brothers met a farmer plowing. He raced home for his log chains.

They lowered the chains and pulled me out just in time. My back and hands were numb.

Cold feet, blisters from holding chain luckily were the ordeal's only effects.

Brink of Death

By C. A. Oswald, Boise, Idaho

On October muley hunt in Idaho's Hell's Canyon country, I got off my horse to toss rocks in small canyon. Three does ran out.

I remounted, and started to cross loose shale when I saw a big buck. In reaching for my rifle, I kicked the horse.

He jumped. Shale started sliding. I went over him, my foot fouled in the stirrup.

We skidded to edge where horse lurched to a halt. I hung over 500-foot drop.

Speaking gently to the wild-eyed, terror-frozen pony, I slowly hauled myself up my own pants leg.

On third try I grabbed rifle scabbard. The horse stayed motionless as I freed my foot.

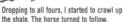

Dropping to all fours, I started to crawl up the shale. The horse turned to follow.

He plunged after me with great leaping bounds. Both of us safe, I thanked God.

Free Loader

By W. Killen, Bettles Field, Alaska

In Alaska's remote John River area, I left my wife near camp to go hunt sheep.

I soon found a fine three-quarter curl Dall, and after tense stalk dropped it.

My .30/06 jammed on reloading, but I decided not to clear it until I'd got the ram back to camp.

Shouldering straps tied to the ram's legs, I set out. Suddenly I felt a tug.

Turning, I saw a grizzly biting the carcass. I gestured wildly.

But the huge beast wouldn't leave. Then I made a desperate move and hit him with my rifle barrel.

The bear struck at me savagely, but I dodged just in time, avoiding certain death. I quickly slipped out of the straps.

Leaving the ram, I ran off, glad to be alive and able to rejoin my wife who otherwise would have been hopelessly stranded.

Close Caller

By Allan Oborne, Alberta

One morning, from my Alberta lookout station, I saw some deer acting jittery partway down the mountain.

I walked down from the cabin to find out why they were uneasy, and had gone 200 yards when I saw a cougar peering at me from behind a boulder.

The big cat showed no sign of backing off. Being unarmed, I picked up a rock.

The cougar came toward me, so I tried to scare it away by throwing the rock at it.

Baring its teeth and growling, the cat came even closer. I turned and ran for the cabin.

The cougar came right after me, and I prayed for wind and strength. Running faster than I ever had, I just made it, the cat at my heels.

As the cougar paced around the cabin, I got a rifle and shot it. Now it's a rug—souvenir of a terrifying ordeal.

Whirlpool

By Carl Mathes, Knoxville, Tennessee

As we fished from a rubber raft beneath Tennessee's Douglas Dam, our motor quit.

Despite frantic paddling, jettisoning gear, we were sucked toward the 135-foot falls.

Ray was going to swim for it, but Del and I grabbed him. Already we were spray-drenched.

As we dipped and bucked in the deafening cascade, Del and I tied Ray to the raft.

Suddenly we shot into the air only to be flung into the water's fury.

We spun in the dam's whirlpool, but I managed to wave my shirt at an angler downriver.

As we flew past one of the cement piers at the dam's base, I made a grab for it.

No go; the beating kept on. Only hope was the angler, who'd left.

Suddenly the torrent was shut off. The angler had reported our plight, and dam guards came to our rescue.

Heroic Terrier

By Floyd E. Warren, Deerwood, Minnesota

One day, as a boy in Nebraska, I was driving my pony and buggy up a road in the hills. My fox terrier was with me.

We were halfway around a ridge when something frightened the pony. She reared up and upset the buggy, hurling me and the dog down the hillside.

Somehow we got entangled, rolling down together for about 20 feet.

Halted by brush, I was appalled to see a huge rattler beside me.

With my face eight inches from its head, I was too terrified even to wink. Suddenly my little dog lunged, grabbed its neck.

The battle was fierce, and the snake was so big it beat the terrier to the ground.

But the dog held the snake till it was dead, its head all but severed.

My terrier had certainly saved my life. The five-foot reptile had 13 rattles and a button.

No Revolving Doors?

By Charley Miller, Bangor, Maine

Shouts brought me quickly to the hunter I was guiding in Maine's Moosehead Lake country. He'd shot a bear at mouth of a low cave.

Only the black's forepart was exposed; the rest was beneath a boulder. We tried to yank him out, but couldn't budge him.

Deciding to push from rear, I crawled between bear's back and top of cave.

My hunter pulled and I pushed, but we made little headway. We agreed to go for help.

As I was squeezing out, the bear came alive, got up, pinned me to top of cave.

Realizing the bear had only been stunned, I yelled to my hunter to shoot it in the chest.

His first shot hit into a paw and drove the bear wild. I nearly died.

When it seemed I couldn't breathe any more, a second shot ended the terrifying ordeal.

Hunters Hunted

By Kermit Roosevelt Jr., New York, New York

Following the steps of my great-grandfather, Teddy Roosevelt, we were after leopard in Africa's Kenya.

We saw one of the cats in the morning, baited a tree, and built a blind. At 2 p.m., when leopards are usually sleeping, we got in the blind to wait.

We were reading. At 4, I looked up and saw the animal crouching six feet away.

We had a rifle and shotgun, and, following whispered advice, I reached for the latter.

As I touched it, the leopard streaked for safety, giving me no time to get in a shot.

As the cat ran, white hunter Terry Matthews said it had likely stalked us for two hours.

Next morning, I got the leopard with one shot from my .264 as he approached the bait. I'm still amazed that he stalked us so successfully the day before.

Fire Escape

By John Skeels, Wray, Colorado

I was only 16 when we were caught in that prairie fire back in 1895. Dad, my brother, and I had been trapping on Oklahoma's Canadian River.

We were north of a hill and did not see the blaze until it roared down around us, almost encircling our wagon.

Our only hope was the river. My brother and I slapped at the mules to get them to jump off the eight-foot bank.

They finally plunged, wagon and all, into seven feet of water. Dad, injured in the Civil War when his ammo wagon turned over, guided us.

The mules were scared to death. We swam and quieted them until they touched bottom near the opposite bank.

Everything was wet, but otherwise in good shape. The river bank was actually an island, on which we stayed and trapped for three weeks.

Armed to the Teeth

By William L. Pepper, New York, New York

Boar hunting in France, I was charged on the trail by one of the pigs. I began firing OO buckshot at 30 yards.

I was hitting the animal with each shot as it came on. At the fifth and last report from my 12 gauge automatic, the brute fell 15 feet from me.

Then, with gun reloaded and safety off, I poked the boar with the muzzle to be sure he was dead.

Before I could press the trigger, the animal grabbed the barrel, wedged a tusk between it and the ventilated rib, and twisted the gun from my hands.

He charged me again, and now, unable to shake off the gun, was literally armed to the teeth.

Realizing I could easily be shot, I leaped on boar with drawn knife.

My blade in the 356-pounder's neck killed him. I show damaged gun to nonbelievers.

Trapper Trapped

By James Leach, La Follette, Tennessee

I approached one of my coon sets in Tacket Creek region of Tennessee, unaware that I had trapped a large bobcat.

When I got within reach, the cat leaped, hit my shoulder, and knocked me over a crevice between the cliff and the ledge I was on.

I fell feet first into the crevice, wedging myself down about seven feet.

The fall broke my right arm. I couldn't defend myself against the screaming cat.

It clawed at my face and neck. I knew my only chance lay in finding some way to reach my gun.

I twisted my body enough to draw the .22 handgun with my left hand.

I was losing a lot of blood from the mauling, but I managed a killing shot.

I fired shots until help came. I was hospitalized for 18 days, but, thank God, I was saved from slow death.

Whirling Terror

By Tony Thompson, Tavernier, Florida

I was fishing one morning in a flat calm off Key Largo, Fla.

Returning, I saw a choppy area on the water about 600 feet from me.

A waterspout was starting! As the spiral cloud formed, I raced toward my dock about a quarter of a mile away.

But, directly in front of the spout, I ran out of gas. No tank was ever filled faster.

As the swirling spout came closer, I yanked on the starter once, and the motor roared to life.

Again I raced for shore, the spout following along behind.

Quickly I tied up at my dock. Meeting the water, the spout resembled a writhing, black barber's pole.

I wanted to watch it, but my feet led me rapidly to my car.

I drove to safety and heard later the spout sucked the flats dry near Tavernier Island.

Bad-Tempered Tusker

By Galen M. Carr, Lubbock, Texas

While visiting a Rhodesian game reserve, I cautiously approached a cow elephant and calf to take a picture.

My guide, Vashko, motioned me to stop when we got within 60 yds. But the huge creature got my scent, and she charged.

Fear made me run as I'd never run before. My lead melted fast.

I fell and the cow was on me. Vashko tried valiantly to distract the beast.

She knelt as if intending to crush me. Her knee grazed my leg, and her hot trunk brushed my back.

Suddenly, a horn blared, and there was my wife, Jo, in our car 6 ft. away. The elephant looked, then rose to her feet.

She ambled off, and I staggered to the car. Vashko later identified the cow as being a notoriously bad-tempered one-tusker.

Olympic Crawl

By Leroy Lewis, Seattle, Washington

Hunting for goat in Washington's Cascades, I spotted a bear but decided not to take him.

Continuing my climb, I started across a snowy ridge at the 7,000-ft. level.

Suddenly, my feet shot out from under me, and I plummeted down a very steep slope.

I tried vainly to slow the fall by jamming my rifle butt into the snow.

Both feet smashed against boulders, and the left one literally exploded.

When I tried to use the rifle as a crutch, I realized my right foot was badly injured, too.

I began to crawl. Twenty hours later, I reached a forest trail.

My knees and ankles were bleeding, so I used two sticks to pull myself along.

Three rangers followed the weird track I had left and found me. They told me I'd crawled five miles.

Two Rides for a Buck

By George Wintz, Creede, Colorado

Hunting in Colorado, I jumped a four-point mule deer and nailed him going away on a hill.

Straddling him, I drew my knife to cut the deer's jugular vein.

But he wasn't dead! I struck, and he leaped down a grade, with me aboard.

I fell off when he hit sliderock below. He ran toward some timber.

The deer lay down some distance away. I picked up gun and knife.

He looked pretty far gone, so I decided there was no need to waste another cartridge on him.

I straddled him, struck him with my knife, and up he went again with me hanging on.

He ran 150 yards and fell, pinning my leg. My knife was gone.

Finally, I managed to open a pocketknife and cut his jugular. I'll never straddle a deer again.

Like a Bat —

By J. L. Cardozo Jr., Sarasota, Florida

My girl, Tiger, was catching all the fish one day near Sarasota, Fla., so I started netting mullet.

As the cast net settled on bottom, the line around my wrist jerked taut.

I was snapped off my feet into the channel and dragged under.

The line slacked, and I fought for the surface, impeded by boots and fish sack.

As I gulped air, the water exploded nearby, and out came a manta ray, a batlike monster with a 9-ft. wingspan. When it plunged back in, it dragged me down again.

"What a stupid way to die," I thought, as I twisted violently through the water.

Suddenly, the line went slack again, and I used my teeth to free the rope.

I clawed for the top, and Tiger, who'd seen it all, paddled madly to my rescue.

Firewater

By H. L. Wilkinson, Stamps, Arkansas

I was taking bass in a creek in a drained-out Lake Erling, Ark., and barely noticed smoke.

About noon, I realized the lake bed was ablaze. Flames leaped across the creek.

I cranked up and headed upstream, hoping to get through before fire cut me off.

Then I sheared a propeller pin. Smoke grew stifling as I put in a spare pin.

I tore off my shirt, wet it, and held it to my face with my eyes uncovered.

Hunching low, I steered into the inferno. Logs sizzled on the surface and flaming limbs fell.

My clothes and skin were smoking, my eyes stung. I couldn't breathe.

I had no idea how much farther I'd have to go. I thought I was doomed.

Suddenly the blaze was behind me. I dropped into the cool water, safe from a fire in the middle of a lake.

Heroic Dog

By Colfax Gregg, as told to Jack McPhee, Coeur d'Alene, Idaho

I dropped a fat moose in the hills back of my cabin in central Alaska.

I quartered it and hung it up since I planned to pack out the meat later.

On a return trip to the cache with my dog Tiger, a grizzly crashed out of the brush and charged me.

The bear grabbed my thigh and threw me down before I could unsling my 9 mm. Mannlicher.

My head banged trees hard as the bear dragged me, but I hung onto my rifle.

The bear dragged me 50 yards, but let go when Tiger rushed up and bit his haunch.

The grizzly turned end-for-end and broke Tiger's spine with one swipe.

I got the rifle up, threw the safety off, and put a bullet through the bear.

The grizzly dropped after running 70 yards. I sadly covered my dog and started out for home.

Moose Meat

By Bill Geagan, Bangor, Maine

When I was a boy, I freighted supplies for a Maine lumber camp with two other boys pulling my "skate."

A blizzard hit, and we carried cargo and skate onto a plowed road to camp.

Moving between banks of snow piled up by a snowplow, we came across a bull moose.

We had to use the road, so we threw some of the cargo at him to frighten him away.

The big bull charged when a heavy horseshoe slammed his left antler.

We scrambled up the snowbank, but the moose ripped my leg. My friends climbed a dead pine.

I kicked the bull and tried to crawl away. The boys threw me a heavy branch.

The moose heard them and turned to butt their tree.

I crawled into the scrub and prayed. I almost froze to death before a passing teamster shot the murderous bull.

In the Soup

By R. F. Slatzer, Columbus, Ohio

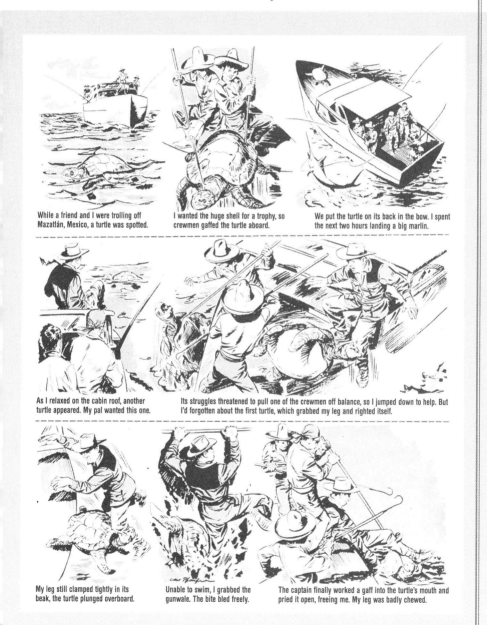

While a friend and I were trolling off Mazatlán, Mexico, a turtle was spotted.

I wanted the huge shell for a trophy, so crewmen gaffed the turtle aboard.

We put the turtle on its back in the bow. I spent the next two hours landing a big marlin.

As I relaxed on the cabin roof, another turtle appeared. My pal wanted this one.

Its struggles threatened to pull one of the crewmen off balance, so I jumped down to help. But I'd forgotten about the first turtle, which grabbed my leg and righted itself.

My leg still clamped tightly in its beak, the turtle plunged overboard.

Unable to swim, I grabbed the gunwale. The bite bled freely.

The captain finally worked a gaff into the turtle's mouth and pried it open, freeing me. My leg was badly chewed.

Yelling Match

By Dick Lasater, Modesto, California

Hunting in Nevada, I shot a mule-deer buck. Two of us gutted it while the other went to our truck for a cart.

We were all bloodied up by the time we got the deer on the cart. Night fell as we hiked along, and we were startled by coyotes yelping nearby.

Then a whole pack began circling us, snarling and yelping—strange behavior for coyotes, we thought.

Sometimes a coyote charged us, but yelling scared it off. We could only yell because my partner had put our rifles in the truck when he went for the cart.

I'm a zoologist and know coyotes don't attack humans, but those snarling animals acted as though they didn't know it.

I don't think they had rabies, but maybe the blood smell masked human scent. When we finally reached the truck, we left fast.

Goat Impasse

By Dave Slutker, Brule, Alberta

I was guiding two hunters in Alberta. One of them shot and hit a big mountain goat.

It was dusk, and we couldn't follow the wounded goat over the mountain.

Next day, we found tracks and blood, but my hunter couldn't make the steep climb.

The goat was dead when Jim Plante, my assistant, and I finally spotted him below us.

Going down, we met another goat on a very narrow ledge.

The goat couldn't turn around, and he bobbed his head angrily. I imagined his 10-inch spikes in my stomach.

I had borrowed my hunter's rifle to finish off his goat, and Jim braced me against the cliff as I fired point-blank.

The recoil didn't knock us off the ledge, but the billy fell dead beside the other one. I'm grateful we came through alive.

Mongrel's Mission

By R. O. Schroeder, Philadelphia, Pennsylvania

It was raining hard as my dad, uncle, and I headed into the mountains of southern Nevada to hunt deer.

Deep in a canyon, the car bogged down in soggy sand of a dry wash.

Not even the horse, which we'd trailered in to pack out deer, could free that car.

Dad decided to ride to a farm 10 miles away to get help. My uncle and I were soon asleep in the auto.

Roused by our dog's barking, we saw water racing down the darkened wash.

We grabbed our guns and sloshed through rising water to higher ground.

Just as we reached safety, a tremendous wall of water roared down the canyon, smashing into car and trailer.

The flash flood hurled the car 500 yards, and the trailer 10 miles, down the canyon. But thanks to that mongrel dog, we were still alive.

Baby and Bear

By Mrs. James Cremin, Circle Pines, Minnesota

While family fished, 9-year-old David babysat for his 7-month-old brother Charles at our campsite.

As the baby sat playing, a bear frightened David into the tent.

As David watched, the bear knocked the log off our cooler and drank the milk.

Suddenly David remembered the baby outside, alone, yet he was too frightened to move out of the tent.

But when the bear walked toward little Charles, David forgot his fear.

After the bear licked the baby's face, David threw a rock at the bear's head.

David ran out as the bear scooped up the child and then hobbled toward the woods.

Our two older boys came back into camp. The bear ran 15 to 20 feet, dropped the baby.

Charles was dirty but unhurt. We got the kids in the car just as the bear came back. Yelling and jumping, we drove him off.

Double Trouble

By Barney Farley, Port Aransas, Texas

Ode Wilson was fishing alone as Ed Cotter and I left launch.

We forgot about Ode as Ed hooked into a wild, leaping, six-foot tarpon.

I gaffed Ed's lively tarpon, and it jumped right into the boat, driving the gaff through its mouth.

As the tarpon landed in the boat, the point of the gaff drove into my leg, knocking me down and pinning me there.

The weight of the thrashing fish on the gaff rope held me down, and Ed couldn't move forward because the bow would have swamped.

We made it to our launch, then saw Ode in trouble.

A giant ray had Ode's anchor line between its feelers and was hauling the bow of his boat down dangerously.

We overtook Ode, and I painfully reached and cut the anchor line.

Fire Trap

By Walker D. Wallace, Fairhope, Alabama

We were trapping at the head of Mobile Bay when fire broke out.

My three partners were out in the marshes, and the wind-driven flames were sweeping down on them. I hurried with our boat.

At Catfish Bayou, I spotted them as they hurried toward the water.

Only two of them made it to the bayou. "Harrington's back there!" they shouted.

When I found him bogged down in the mire, the flames were racing at us.

The wind drove a wall of flame toward the bayou as I carried my exhausted friend to the boat.

I put him down, removed the boat's motor, and told the others to help me turn the boat upside down with one gunwale on the bank.

We propped the boat with oars and dragged Harrington underneath it.

Submerging as much as possible in the neck-deep water, we felt the oncoming fire leap the bayou.

As fast as it came, the wall of fire raced away. We offered up our thanks.

Boarding Party

By Bob Miller, as told to Ed Baggett, Fort Pierce, Florida

I was trolling off Bethel Shoals with my clients Bob Safford and Gary Tilton.

Suddenly the rod in the port holder bent double, and Gary was into a strong wahoo. Bob reeled in.

I knew the fight would attract sharks, and we soon saw a fin.

Up close, I struck at hammerhead, drove the sharp gaff into his nose.

Trying to disengage the gaff, I stumbled backward, pulling on the gaff handle to keep my balance as I fell. The thrashing, six-foot shark came crashing right into the boat.

Keeping out of range of the shark's snapping teeth, I grabbed his tail.

Afraid to let go and afraid to hold on, I lifted at the right moment; the shark flipped itself out.

Wahoo safe in the fish box and our gear smashed, we called it a day.

Snake Pit

By Axel Jonasson, San Jose, California

Four of us were shooting on my California ranch when I gave in to the lure of an abandoned mine.

Deciding to explore one large shaft, I started down but soon lost control.

A small ledge 50 ft. below was my only hope, but I bounced off of it and soared into the gaping hole.

Incredibly, after a flight of 40 ft. I landed uninjured on a second ledge.

But my troubles weren't over. A chilling sound made me turn and see a rattler not 4 ft. away.

Sketch shows mine's setup. The main shaft split below my ledge.

I hollered up to my friends for help, and they threw down a revolver wrapped snugly in a coat.

Though trembling, I managed to shoot the still coiled snake.

Summoned by my friends, some forest rangers arrived with a winch-equipped truck and lowered cable to me.

Though a sharp, upthrust rock was a danger, my luck—and the cable—held.

Buck's Ambush

By Mrs. Rose Warren, Mountlake Terrace, Washington

My brother Lee was tracking a wounded buck, and the sign indicated he was getting near.

Suddenly, from 10 feet away, wounded buck leaped. It knocked Lee down, throwing his rifle out into the brush.

The buck turned. With antlers flying, it viciously gored him. Then the buck started flailing him with its three good legs.

Hanging desperately to buck's antlers, Lee managed to work his pocketknife open but cut his hand in process.

Before Lee could strike with the knife, the buck made another wild leap and jerked him off the ground and loosened his hold.

As buck turned to gore him again, Lee regained his hold around animal's neck and drove knife deep, severing jugular vein.

Blood flowed, and deer collapsed and died on top of Lee. Badly gored, bruised, and cut, Lee felt lucky to be alive.

Stampede!

By Claude Elmore, Anchorage, Alaska

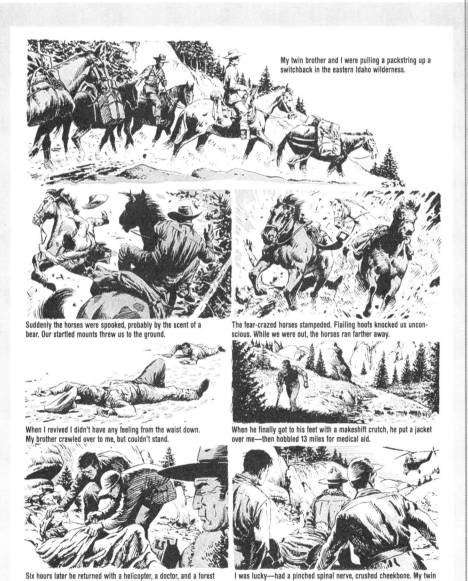

My twin brother and I were pulling a packstring up a switchback in the eastern Idaho wilderness.

Suddenly the horses were spooked, probably by the scent of a bear. Our startled mounts threw us to the ground.

The fear-crazed horses stampeded. Flailing hoofs knocked us unconscious. While we were out, the horses ran farther away.

When I revived I didn't have any feeling from the waist down. My brother crawled over to me, but couldn't stand.

When he finally got to his feet with a makeshift crutch, he put a jacket over me—then hobbled 13 miles for medical aid.

Six hours later he returned with a helicopter, a doctor, and a forest ranger. I was given first aid before they moved me.

I was lucky—had a pinched spinal nerve, crushed cheekbone. My twin had torn knee cartilages, but his hike had saved me.

Striped Ambush

By L/Cpl. Jim Shepherd, U.S.M.C.,
as told to 2nd Lt. R. L. Drieslein, U.S.M.C.

I was the point man on a Marine Corps ambush patrol sent out past our lines at night in jungle near the DMZ in Vietnam.

Tigers had stalked our patrols at a distance several times. Now one sneaked past my patrol leader and headed my way.

Then the big cat sprang, catching me completely by surprise. In the wild scuffle, I dropped my M16 rifle and it was gone.

The tiger soon overpowered me and bit into my left arm. Then it began dragging me toward a small stream about 10 feet away.

Somehow I reared up, punching the cat in the face with my right hand, stunning it.

My buddies hearing the commotion ran to my aid, scaring off the big tiger.

They carried me to our unit; then I was sent to a rear-base hospital to recover.

Cat Fight

By Pat Malone, as told to Ed Hicks, Fort Smith, Arkansas

Floating in an inner tube in 20 feet of water, I was using a spinning rig on the Fourche La Fave River near Waldron, Arkansas. I cast a grasshopper near a tree.

I got a jolting strike. For a half-hour that fish towed me around and I hung on.

When I fought it to the surface, the big cat, spikes erect, butted into my tube.

Next he flipped against the tube and whacked me in the head with his tail.

Then he went deep. I was afraid that he would tangle my legs in line or rip tube.

I got the fish back up and tried to put him on my stringer. The hook popped out.

As I thrust my hands into his jaws, he clamped down, his big tail flailing.

Badly scraped, I landed the 33-pounder as my wife came on the peaceful scene.

Smash-Up!

By Richard T. Hankel, Chicago, Illinois

While on a hunt for big game in Mozambique, I shot at a Cape buffalo about 150 yards away with a double-barrel Holland & Holland .470 and wounded him.

The animal ran into some high grass and disappeared. We had to go in after him.

My white hunter and I got separated as we searched for the injured buff.

Suddenly I heard a noise. I spun to see the bull charging 30 feet away.

I had time for one shot. I hit the buff in the chest, but his great momentum . . .

. . . catapulted him right into me. He smashed my hip, knocking me down, then rolled over dead beside me. My white hunter ran up to find me . . .

. . . writhing in pain, my hip bone pulverized. Now I have a metal hip and must walk with two canes.

138

Bayonet Charge

By Cecil McGraw, as told to Sock Clay, Portsmouth, Ohio

I was moving cautiously along a low ridge in southern Ohio, looking for a squirrel that I could hear cutting in a nearby tree.

As I eased over a rotten log a horde of angry yellow jackets suddenly swarmed up from the ground and covered me all over.

There seemed to be thousands of the insects. They got into my eyes, clothes, and shoes and under my hat and kept stinging.

I ran downhill through heavy brush, but the faster I ran the more they stung me.

The Little Scioto River was nearby; I made a dash for it and dived in.

I stayed under a long time, but when I came up there were still there—and mad.

I went down again and this time swam a few yards underwater. The tactic worked.

As I pulled myself out I was shaking and nauseated, but I finally made . . .

. . . it back to my truck. I had over 100 stings and was ill from them for a week.

Escape by a Nose

By Don Fletcher, Grasmere, British Columbia,
as told to Bob Steindler

A hunter I was guiding in British Columbia shot a grizzly in the shoulder. It ran off, and we tracked it to a pine thicket.

The bear charged out. My hunter emptied his rifle at it, but it kept coming. I was unarmed but tried to distract . . .

. . . the bear while my hunter reloaded. It took out after me, and I ran. But 20 feet away I tripped and the bear was on me.

I tried to roll out of the way, but the bear clamped down on my right leg.

I grabbed his nose and twisted it hard, and he let go. Then he went for my . . .

. . . head. I lost the nose grip but got hold of his lower jaw and wrenched it.

When my hand slipped I fended off his jaws by punching his nose repeatedly.

My hunter had reloaded and finally got a clear shot. The bear collapsed on me.

I almost blacked out, but we made it to my truck. My knee took 40 stitches.

Firewater

By *Kenneth E. Allen, Trumann, Arkansas*

Four of us had been hunting ducks from our blind on the St. Francis River near Trumann, Arkansas. We got our limits, then started home in our aluminum boat.

It was very cold; snow and sleet got so thick that visibility became almost nil.

We hit a log, shearing a motor pin. I had no extra pin, so we had to paddle.

We lit a charcoal bucket to warm our hands, unaware that the tipped-up . . .

. . . motor was leaking gas. Suddenly fire flared. We went overboard, guns and all.

We managed to tip the leaking motor down, and the fire finally went out.

We got back into the boat and paddled to the nearest blind, where a fire . . .

. . . was still burning. After warming up, we found a nail to serve as a shear pin.

No Pictures, Mister!

By Bob Theisen, Deerfield, Illinois

After a hunt on which I'd shot a polar bear, I was in the general store in Teller, Alaska, when an Eskimo with a sled team raced past. I wanted to . . .

. . . film them, so I grabbed my movie camera and gave chase. They stopped about 600 . . .

. . . yards away, and I caught up. The Eskimo agreed to let me take a few pictures, so I got out in front and began filming.

Before either of us realized it, the team changed directions and came straight toward me. I kept filming, and suddenly . . .

. . . I was on the ground with 11 half-starved huskies on top of me and biting me all over.

I yelled as their teeth sank into my flesh. The Eskimo kept trying to pull the dogs off. Finally, I managed to crawl out from under the frenzied pack.

I got up, grabbed my camera, and ran in a daze toward my quonset 500 yards away.

Luckily people with medical training were around. They stitched my wounds.

Then I was flown to a hospital for more stitches. Later, I got 14 rabies shots.

Watch Out Below!

By Wayne Drapak, Fort William, Ontario

Last winter I was heading for a lake in the Spruce River Road area north of Fort William, Ontario, to do some ice fishing.

As I was walking along I heard what sounded like a cry or a moan above me.

Just as I looked up a lynx leaped out of a tree onto my face. I reached . . .

. . . up and grabbed the cat and flung him to the ground. Then I threw off my . . .

. . . mittens and quickly got hold of his throat with my bare hands. My only thought was to kill him before he killed me.

I felt the cat's razor-sharp claws tearing at my face, legs, and hands. I tried to pin his front legs down with my elbows.

Then, on an impulse, I swung him hard against a tree trunk. That action . . .

. . . only stunned the lynx long enough for me to regain my grip on his neck.

I finally killed him but suffered many deep cuts. Fortunately, he wasn't rabid.

Dive Bombers

By Jack Turner, Lonesome Lake, British Columbia

While hunting alone in the West Kootenay area of British Columbia I spotted some goats on a mountain across a deep valley.

To stalk them I had to cross the valley, climb a steep slope, and inch across a narrow ledge.

I had eased about 50 feet along the 150-foot ledge when I heard an eerie piercing scream and felt the thudding of huge wings directly behind me.

I turned my head and saw a large bald eagle flying out over the canyon. Before I could recover from my shocked surprise a second eagle dived . . .

. . . down angrily at me from above. It came right at my head, talons extended, and then swerved . . .

. . . aside at the last moment. I lost all interest in goats, and edged my way back. The birds swooped at me all the way.

When I got off the ledge, they left me and landed about 20 feet above the spot of the first attack, where I now saw a nest.

Curiosity Misfires

By Roland Gebauer, Kelowna, British Columbia

My father-in-law and I had driven up Blue Grouse Mountain near Kelowna, B. C., and then hiked a mile to the top. On the way back, something made me turn around.

A cougar crouched 10 feet behind us, ready to spring. I threw my camera . . .

. . . at the cat and accidentally knocked my father-in-law off his feet. The cougar kept coming. My father-in-law scrambled up fast, and I picked up a fallen tree.

I hit the cat over the head with the tree, but that didn't discourage him.

He kept following us while we moved steadily down the road. From time . . .

. . . to time we threw rocks and pieces of wood at the cat. Finally, after half . . .

. . . a mile, he moved off. Nervous and watchful, we made it back to the car.

Boar Charge

By Phillip Ludwig, Kissimmee, Florida

My 11-year-old son Chris and I each had arrowed a wild boar on a preserve near Galena, Illinois.

Chris stayed on top of a hill to admire his trophy while I walked down with a friend to see his boar. Suddenly I heard a terrified cry, "Dad!"

I turned and saw Chris running full-tilt downhill just ahead of a charging boar.

I drew my hunting knife and headed uphill toward them. As Chris and . . .

. . . I passed each other I dropped to my knees, knife extended toward the boar.

The angry animal came on but at the last second swerved to the side, barely missing the point of the knife. Then he ran off into the brush.

Chris, pale and shaken, had to lie on the ground awhile to recuperate from the scare of a lifetime.

Hunter's Downfall

By Delbert Dawson, Murray, Utah

I was packing out a two-point buck that I'd shot near Mt. Nebo in Utah, when I came to a 20-foot falls. Trying to pick my way down the cliff, I made a misstep.

As I fell I shoved the deer aside and grabbed for brush, but I got only air.

I hit under the falls with a jolt and felt the deer crash down on top of me.

Dazed, I crawled out. The iciness of the water made me feel numb all over.

I managed to drag the buck out of the churning pool. Then I was running . . .

. . . for my truck. Brush clawed at me, and I fought a powerful urge to sleep.

It was dark when I reached the truck. I drank whiskey and coffee, then . . .

. . . changed into dry clothing. I was so numb I had to slice my boot laces off.

Fire and Ice

By R. W. Raymer, Frobisher Bay, Northwest Territories

My Eskimo partner Eliyah Nowdlak and I were hunting seals near Frobisher Bay in Canada's Northwest Territories when we spotted a snow squall sweeping toward us.

We abandoned the stalk and raced back to an old igloo in our snow machines.

I unpacked gear while Eliyah patched up the snowhouse. We lit candles and a . . .

. . . stove, sealed the entrance, and had tea. When I spread my bag we found . . .

. . . that gas had saturated it. Before we could act, the fumes ignited in . . .

. . . a blinding explosion. Frantically we burst a hole in the igloo and dived out.

The igloo melted fast as we salvaged as much gear as possible with a gaff.

Scorched and shivering, we loaded the sleds and headed the many miles home.

Claim Jumper

By Dan Bascello, Thunder Bay Station, Ontario

I was duck hunting with my brother and a friend at a beaver dam about 18 miles from Thunder Bay, Ontario.

Three mallards flew toward me, then flared off, but . . .

. . . I dropped one on dry ground to my right. As I walked over to . . .

. . . retrieve it, I saw what had made the birds flare. A lynx . . .

. . . had claimed my downed duck, and he wouldn't back off. I yelled to scare . . .

. . . him off, but he kept advancing. I raised my gun to fire. It jammed, and I had no . . .

. . . knife. I called for help just as the snarling cat pounced on me, clawing at my chest and shoulder and knocking me to . . .

. . . the ground. After a struggle I managed to get up and throw the animal off of me. Just then my friend, who . . .

. . . had heard my yells, arrived and shot the cat. Though my heavy clothing had protected me, I still have scars from . . .

. . . the fracas. Lynx normally are timid, but hunger must have prodded this one. He stretched out to almost five feet long.

The Big Crunch

By Dennis Corrington, Nome, Alaska

In May, after the ice began to go out in the Bering Sea near my home in Nome, Alaska, I took my 12-foot sailboat out to hunt seals.

As I tacked between two large ice pans, I failed to notice that they were converging until I heard a . . .

. . . crunching noise behind me. Seeing that I was fast being caught in the closing rise, I dropped sail and tried to . . .

. . . motor the two-mile distance to the outside edge of the pans with my small outboard. I wasn't fast enough. The . . .

. . . walls of ice began to pull the boat stern-first into the crack. I cut the safety line and released the motor. The . . .

. . . ice sucked it down. All water disappeared, and the ice heaved upward, pushing the boat out of the crushing jaws.

I leaped out and manhandled the boat to keep it out from under the toppling car-size ice chunks.

After five minutes the pans became silent. I pulled . . .

. . . the boat to the edge of the ice and, after making minor repairs, sailed home.

Double Jeopardy

By Henry Nystrand, Mexico City, Mexico

I was hunting jungle cock on a narrow trail in dense jungle in central India. My young guide Shanka was leading the way.

Suddenly I heard a bloodcurdling scream. Two furious sloth bears appeared on the trail 10 yards ahead of us and charged.

Shanka turned and fled past me. Instinctively I raised my drilling, which had a .30/06 cartridge in the lower barrel.

I had no time to aim. I just pointed the gun at the closest bear and fired. He dropped as if clubbed. The other bear . . .

. . . was momentarily blocked but circled to my right to get at me. My drilling had only a birdshot shell in the left . . .

. . . barrel and a .22 in the right. I ran into the jungle and frantically pulled a buckshot shell from my cartridge holder.

I could hear the bear screaming and crashing as I loaded the gun, but . . .

. . . soon the noise faded. I looked for Shanka and found him high in a slim . . .

. . . tree. We returned to Mandikhera and got an oxcart to retrieve the dead bear.

Bear Trap

By John Suda, Greenwood, Wisconsin

In the fall of 1968, I was hunting black bear in northern Wisconsin. Our six dogs hit a scent and eventually bayed the bear in a tag-elder swamp.

I got to the scene and, when I had an opening, shot the bear in the chest with my .308 rifle.

The huge bear fell but was still alive and snapping at the attacking hounds. My dog was near the bear's head and in danger, so I ran up to pull him away.

Suddenly the bear reared up. I turned to run but had made only one step when the . . .

. . . bear caught my boot heel in his mouth and I fell. The next thing I knew, the . . .

. . . enraged animal was astraddle me, snarling and swatting at . . .

. . . the dogs. As they held his attention, I crawled out from under him and ran . . .

. . . but fell again. One partner arrived and shot, but the bear wouldn't drop.

As it rose up to lunge at me, another partner shot it. The bear toppled . . .

. . . over, dead. Its undressed weight was 530 pounds. Amazingly, I wasn't injured.

Crash Landing

By Mrs. John H. Meyer, Austin, Texas

My husband and I were driving along a ranch road in central Texas when we saw a whitetail doe on a ledge next to the road.

As we approached the deer at about 35 m.p.h., she panicked and tried to jump over our pickup truck. She didn't make it.

I screamed as the deer crashed through the windshield on my side and landed in the cab, spattering me with glass. My . . .

. . . face and neck were badly cut and I was dazed, but I asked my husband . . .

. . . to drive on for help. I passed out several times before he found a motel.

As he ran in for help, the deer, which we had assumed was dead, began to move.

My husband came back and pulled the struggling doe out of the cab. She . . .

. . . staggered off. Then he and a motel guest carried me inside for first . . .

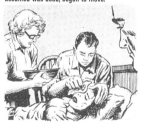

. . . aid. Later I went to a hospital. I still have scars from the freak accident.

Moose Block

By Larry Baxter, Whitney Point, New York

While stationed in Alaska, my wife and I were avid dog mushers. One night we were running a team around our training trail.

As we rounded a fast curve, I saw a huge form blocking our . . .

. . . path. It was a moose. I stamped frantically on the sled's brake and dragged my other foot, trying to avert a collision, but the seven excited huskies lunged forward. The . . .

. . . moose bolted and trampled my two wheel dogs. Other dogs slashed at his belly while my lead dog tried to obey and pull us all away from the melee.

I dumped my wife into a snowbank and looked for an escape route, but she was pregnant . . .

. . . and could hardly move in the deep snow banking the trail. The moose solved our problem by charging right by us, so . . .

. . . close that I could have punched him. I helped my wife back into the sled and mushed the team back to the the kennels.

Hot Rod

By Mabe Davidson, Fayetteville, Arkansas

I was trout fishing on the Eleven Point River in southern Missouri when I came to a spot where I had to climb a steep bank.

Carrying my rod in one hand, I grabbed for roots and rocks to pull myself up.

Suddenly my hand grasped something soft. It thrashed, and I jerked . . .

. . . my hand back frantically. I'd grabbed a copperhead but miraculously had not . . .

. . . been bitten. He was still in my way, so I poked him with my rod tip. As he . . .

. . . jerked away, my lure hooked his tail. He tried to get at me as I . . .

. . . held the rod far out and climbed to the top. Then I killed him with a rock.

Bump and Run

By Garth Winger, Millersburg, Pennsylvania

While I was working at a mission in Zambia, an African was injured by a Cape buffalo. I rounded up two guns and six . . .

. . . other men and went out to hunt it. We found its tracks and followed them. Suddenly the buff appeared and charged.

I raised my rifle, but before I could release the safety the buff was almost on me. I dodged. He sailed by me and . . .

. . . headed for my partner who had the other gun and who was not far behind me. The huge animal bowled him over and . . .

. . . continued on toward our bush vehicle parked on the road. We hollered, and . . .

. . . the driver hopped into the car. The buff stopped, then charged the car . . .

. . . and smashed into the front bumper. Then he backed off and hit it again . . .

. . . and again. I had released my safety and finally got a broadside shot at . . .

. . . about 50 yards. The big bull went down but tried to get up again. I . . .

. . . shot twice more and finished him—the first Cape buffalo I'd ever seen.

156

Vision of Death

By David D. Martin, Seattle, Washington

On a backpack fishing trip in high country with my dog, I was wearing new bifocal glasses, and it was hard to see whenever I looked down at the ground. Maybe that . . .

. . . caused my fall. My glasses flew off. I dropped my rod and got rid of the ax.

I hurtled down a smooth rock face with my pack still on my back. I was sure . . .

. . . I'd be killed, but then my heels hit a ledge hard. I stood there trying . . .

. . . not to panic. My toes hung over a big drop, and my legs and feet hurt. The . . .

. . . pack made it hard to move, so I got it off but hung onto it. After a . . .

. . . breather, I inched my way painfully along the ledge toward some bushes . . .

. . . and the slope grew less steep. My faithful dog was waiting when I got . . .

. . . to the top. My right foot hurt very much, so I cut a staff and hobbled . . .

. . . toward my car. With half a mile to go, I was bushed, but then I met a . . .

. . . family. The man helped me out, and I drove to my home with a broken foot.

Hippo Hangup

By Jaclynn Browneye, Grand Rapids, Michigan

We were camping in west Africa. After dark I went to get the boys, who were fishing, and we headed back.

Suddenly, in brush beside the narrow path, something snorted, and the lantern showed a hippo a few feet away.

Jim's lure snagged on Paul's pants as they lit out. Terrified, I started to run back down toward the river.

Dave stopped me, but tripped and dropped his lantern. He grabbed his flashlight as the hippo loomed over us.

Dave raced up the hill toward the camp. I was so scared that I ran right past them all, as white as a ghost.

Paul and Jim came trotting in—carefully—behind me. The hippo, about as confused as we were, lumbered off.

Grizzly in the Dooryard

By Mrs. David R. Gratias, Anchorage, Alaska

I was staying in our cabin near Denali, Alaska, with our baby Theresa and our 180-pound St. Bernard dog.

There was a noise outside, and the dog and I went to investigate. I left the door open.

We call our dog Grizzly Bear because he's so big and heavy, and I thought of that when I almost ran into a grizzly cub.

Because I knew the sow had to be nearby, I turned to run for the open door but came face to face with the old bear.

The sow lunged, and I fell. She raked my cheek with one paw and sank claws into my shoulder. Just as she was mouthing . . .

. . . my upper arm, our dog crashed into the bear like a battering ram. They began to fight, but I blacked out.

When I came to, the dog was licking my face. The bear and cub were gone. There was blood on the dog, but he was . . .

. . . not hurt, so it must have been mine or the bear's. Our gentle giant won three awards for his surprising bravery.

Bout with Rut-Crazed Buck

By Richard Schmidt, Williams, Arizona

On a November trip to Walnut Canyon, Ariz., my wife, my mother, and I visited ancient Indian cave dwellings.

Hiking out of the canyon, we were met by a mule-deer buck that blocked the trail.

The mulie was acting odd, so I told the ladies to climb a rock. I did the same when the buck charged.

With nostrils flared and hair on end, the buck jumped onto the rock and tried to gore me. I grabbed his rack and twisted his head aside.

We tumbled off the rock, but I still held onto the crazed buck. I told the ladies to run up the trail.

They made it to the museum, and my mother collapsed. Rangers showed up, and my wife frantically told them what was happening.

When they arrived, I was exhausted and the buck had me pinned. The rangers hit the buck with their hats until it backed off.

Obviously in rut, the buck finally left, but he did not hurry. It was a bruising ordeal I'll never forget.

A Very Unfunny Joke

By Steve Kohler, Lake Charles, Louisiana

My buddy Jerry and I had built duck blinds in a bayou and were going home, his boat towing mine.

He decided to play a joke on me and towed me over a gator hole that he knew was occupied.

When Jerry cut the motor, the big alligator slapped the boat with her tail and suddenly lunged for me.

The gator grabbed the boat in her jaws, just missing my hand. Her teeth came through the boat's bottom, and water began to rush in.

With teeth lodged in the boat, the gator couldn't get her jaws loose. She thrashed around wildly, and I was sinking.

Jerry tried to start the motor, but it flooded. He began to pole frantically to get me clear of the gator hole.

At last my boat moved and the gator shook its grip loose. Water still rushed into my 14-ft. aluminum boat.

Jerry barely made it to a dock. His practical joke had backfired. The incident was our fault; gators seldom attack unless threatened.

Attacked by Bobcats

By Wm. Dachenhausen, Ruby, New York

I was about to get a shot at a deer in a New York forest when some bark fell from a hemlock overhead.

Then, something jumped onto my back and I struggled to shake free—it was a bobcat!

I hit the cat with the side of my gun, knocking him to the ground. Dazed, I stepped back to get room for a shot.

Before I could fire, two more bobcats jumped from the same tree. I managed to shoot them both as they hit the ground.

By this time the first cat had recovered from the blow I'd given him and was coming at me again. I quickly fired and dropped him. Ringed by the three dead cats, I heard a noise and I swung around just in time to see a fourth bobcat.

I fired and kept on shooting until my Winchester was emptied. In utter disbelief I looked around for more cats.

Satisfied there were no more, I slumped to the ground wondering what they could've done to an unarmed man.

162

Bat Attack

By James Ibbison III, Westerly, Rhode Island

One night on a Rhode Island beach after work, I saw signs for good early morning bass fishing.

I slept until 2:00 a.m., then got up, grabbed my tackle, and drove back to the dark moonless beach.

I climbed down on some rocks with my tackle. But as I cast out into the surf, I suddenly saw bats circling over my head.

I reeled my plug in fast, but the bats swooped and dived at my head. One knocked my cap off; I swung to defend myself.

In terror, I threw down my rod and ran for my jeep, but the bats chased me as I ran. It was like a horror movie come true.

My heart pounded as I climbed to safety in my jeep. I waited for the bats to leave so I could get my gear.

When I opened the door to retrieve my tackle, the bats began to dive at me again. Later, I got my gear and drove home.

I had been bitten on my ear. Next day at the hospital, I got my first rabies shot in a long and painful series.

Mad, Mad Moose

By Dana Weat, Portage, Maine

One October, I was at an outfitter's camp in northern Maine for late-season fly fishing.

As I walked to my canoe, I was suddenly confronted by a bull moose in full rut, pawing the sand.

The moose charged me. I dropped my tackle and ran as fast as I could for my cabin.

I barely made it to the cabin. Just as I ran through the door, the rut-crazed bull thundered onto the porch only a few feet behind me.

I slammed the cabin door shut, but I wasn't safe yet. The huge moose attacked the door, banging and splintering it with his rack again and again, trying to knock it down. My heart pounded when he looked as if he might succeed.

Finally, the moose gave up. He walked away, glaring at me over his shoulder. Then he disappeared in the woods.

When it was safe, I retrieved my fishing gear and examined the damaged door. I felt lucky to have escaped the enraged moose.

Killer Bear

By Peter Talbot, Seattle, Washington

I was on a fall camping trip with three friends in Glacier Bay, Alaska, in an area that rangers told us a camper had been reported missing. We arrived on the day boat, then set out to make camp.

At our camp a brown bear suddenly came at us. We banged on pans to scare him away.

When the big bear didn't stop, we started running for safer ground.

From across a small lake, we watched as the bear ripped our camp gear apart.

Then the bear charged, ignoring our food. We ran for our lives through the brush.

The chase ended on a gravel hill with the bear 10 feet away. He stopped in surprise as we began to shout and throw rocks at him.

The bear backed down, and we waited in fear for an hour. We decided one of us had to stay if he charged us again.

Finally he left. When we hiked to the beach, we learned that the missing camper had been found, eaten by a bear.

Pinned by an Elk

By Donald Patton, Madison, Wisconsin

My son David and I were in a Wisconsin game preserve, helping the owner with a special project.

Without warning, I was suddenly confronted by the reserve's snorting, dehorned elk.

The elk charged, so I jumped behind a tree, shouting to scare him away.

My hip boots were awkward, but I tried to escape by climbing.

Then the elk hit my legs, knocking me down and smashing my ribs with his blunt horns.

Desperately, I plunged my knife in his neck. David had heard my cries and came running with a log.

Dave hit the elk's head with the log but the elk was unfazed. Then the furious elk charged David, knocking him over a stump.

I pulled the weakening elk from David, but he charged me again. This time, I grabbed his ears as he got close.

Finally, the elk collapsed and died. My son and I were safe, but later I found out that I had 11 broken ribs.

Night of the Bear

By Paul Cameron, Dearborn, Michigan

One weekend, while I was on a camping trip in a Michigan state park, I was awakened by growling outside my pup tent. Suddenly, a bear started clawing at my tent, trying to knock it down.

Without warning, the bear bit me through the tent, dragging me about and cracking the bones in my arm.

As the bear knocked my tent down, I rolled outside on the ground. I played dead, hoping the bear would lose interest and leave.

But the bear attacked again, biting my neck and lifting me off the ground.

When the bear dropped me, I ran hard for the nearest big tree.

The bear climbed the tree after me. It looked as if there were no escape.

In desperation, I leaped to a nearby tree. From there, I watched as the bear climbed down and walked out of sight.

Some passing motorists helped me down. Later, in the hospital, I learned rangers found the bear and shot it.

Hammerhead Havoc

By Bob Stearns, Miami, Florida

I was fishing with my good friend Chico in the Florida Keys when he hooked a 100-pound tarpon on his fly rod.

During the fight, the tarpon towed us into deeper water, a mile offshore.

The fish fought wildly when a huge hammerhead shark appeared just off our lightweight, 15-foot boat and attacked the fish.

I threw our 16-foot pushpole at the shark as it zeroed in on our boat. The pole bounced off the 12-foot hammerhead's back, causing it to swerve away.

I reclaimed the pole and rammed it against the shark as it attacked again, turning it.

I took advantage of the shark's confusion, grabbed the exhausted tarpon by the gill plates and hauled it up.

We quickly left the area for shallow water before the shark returned. I held the tarpon until it recovered and freed it.

Killer Dog Pack

By David Richey, Buckley, Michigan

I was fishing along Michigan's Sturgeon River when three big dogs attacked me.

I quickly hit the lead dog, a German shepherd, across the muzzle with my flyrod.

The rod broke, but I kept slashing at the dog with the tip. It backed away, but the others moved in.

The other German shepherd and a Collie kept trying to circle me from behind. I kept facing them, knowing I had to avoid being pulled down.

I reached for a branch just as two dogs came at me. I fought them off desperately with my rod and limb.

The shepherd's teeth shredded my rod, and the Collie bit through my waders and into my lower leg, as I tried clubbing them off.

I knocked the Collie unconscious, and then ran for the river as the two shepherds chased me.

When I got into the water, the dogs ran off. Later, the dogs' owner agreed to keep them penned up, but only when I threatened a lawsuit.

Trapped in Hidden Well

By Steve Lovin, Aliceville, Alabama

While deer hunting in Alabama, I decided to explore an area covered with thick vines.

Suddenly, without warning, I lost my balance, falling into an abandoned well over 30 feet deep.

As I landed in waist-deep muck and water, a board I had knocked loose hit me on the head.

Dazed, I flicked on my lighter and decided that my only way out was to dig hand holds into the clay walls with my knife. I tied my rifle to my waist.

I began climbing, but my wet clothes and boots made it nearly impossible.

I was about halfway up when my legs cramped, causing me to crash back into the water. Exhausted, hurt, and cold, I knew I had to get out on my next attempt.

I again began to inch my way up the wall, despite the horrible pain in my muscles.

Finally, I reached the surface. Still confused, I stumbled to my truck and drove to a hospital, where several wood splinters were removed from my scalp.

Dragged Under by a Fish

By Emiliano Feliberti, Hato Rey, Puerto Rico

I was fishing with my son off Puerto Rico when he hooked a huge kingfish, 400 yards out.

I was about to wire and gaff the fish when I fell in, holding the wire close to its mouth.

One of the two bait hooks pierced my finger, the line broke, and the fish started dragging me down.

I was drowning, and I knew my only chance was to rip the other bait hook out of the fish's mouth. I frantically groped for it.

As the kingfish's teeth tore my hand, I finally got the original hook out of its mouth, and was loose.

I desperately shot upward with my last reserve of energy. Nearly unconscious, I reached the surface and took in air.

Though I popped up 50 yards away from the boat, my son quickly reached me and threw me a rope and a life buoy.

Another boatload of people rescued me, and cut the hook out of my finger. Though in shock, I recovered quickly.

Death Leap

By William Linney, Churchville, New York

One late fall evening, I was raccoon hunting with my friend, Kelly Adams, near Churchville, New York. Our three hounds eventually picked up a strong scent, and were soon chasing a coon.

The dogs drove the big boar into a tree along the banks of Black Creek.

I leashed the dogs and held on to them along the bank's edge.

Kelly shot the animal with a .22. It was a solid hit, but the coon was still alive.

Cornered and crazed, the desperate boar ran out on a limb and jumped out of the tree.

I never saw the 30-pound coon come out of the darkness. With a loud crash, it struck my head and neck, knocking me unconscious and into the water.

I sank to the bottom, and would have drowned if Kelly wasn't there to save me. The coon died where it hit me.

I swallowed a lot of water and my head throbbed. At the hospital, doctors found I had broken my shoulder and cracked a vertebra.

Tarpon I Didn't Want

By Lamar Underwood, New York, New York

My friend Tom and I were tarpon fishing in Parismania River, Costa Rica. We used separate, guided boats to photograph each other playing fish. Suddenly, Tom yelled that he had hooked a big one.

I laid down my rod, and reached for my camera; Tom was 50 yards away.

As I picked up the camera, Tom yelled, "Look out!" I was shocked to see his line sawing through the water right at me, only about five feet from my boat.

In one incredible leap, the tarpon soared through the air, twisting and turning. He hit me broadside, his head landing on my right foot, his body and tail hitting me head-on. The collision knocked me right out of the boat.

As I surfaced, the fish was still thrashing wildly in the boat. My guide desperately tried to avoid it.

Had he landed the fish, Tom would have released it. Instead, it died in the boat. I had a broken foot, and spent weeks on crutches.

House Guest

By Bernie J. Full, Cannon City, Colorado

I was cutting Christmas trees in the Rockies when a sudden snowstorm struck the high country. My pick up truck bogged down when I tried to get away, so I slogged through the snow to a line shack.

Safe inside the shack, I started a fire, ate some of the canned food, and eventually drifted off to sleep.

Scuffling noises woke me. The light from the fire was dim, but I could see. Then something dropped from the loft with a thud.

A mountain lion was near the door. Every time I moved, he tensed. We played cat and mouse the rest of the night.

By moving very slowly, I managed to get hold of the ax and most of my clothes. I slid the window open and squirmed out.

It was a clear morning, and I ran for my truck. When I looked back, the cat was following along about 100 yards behind.

A plane alerted by my wife found me, and its engine noise drove the cat off. The pilot radioed a jeep to pick me up.

Trapped in My Own Trap

By Stan Madsen, as told to Charlie Kroll, Grayling, Michigan

My beaver sets were the "quick-drowning" kind. A trapped beaver makes for deep water. and the trap chain slides down a wire staked in the stream. The slide isn't reversible, so the beaver drowns.

High water and ice knocked one of my traps into deeper water. Nothing was in the trap, but I had to get it back.

I didn't have a trap hook, so I grabbed a sapling and slid my hand down the trap wire, hoping to reach the trap chain.

I slipped and fell, still holding onto the sapling. Then my foot hit the pan (trigger), and the leg-hold closed on my instep.

My hand lost its grip on the sapling. I was freezing, and the current pushed me down. I knew I'd drown.

I made a lunge and got hold of a limb, but the trap held me with my face just above the foaming stream.

Fear gave me power. With one heave, I pulled the stake out and flopped onto the bank. From now on, I'll have a long trap hook.

Deaf to Danger

By R. H. Harrold, Auburn, Washington

I was walking a railroad trestle back to my car after an unsuccessful try for steelhead. A freight train came from behind me, and I didn't hear it because of the cap and hood snugged over my ears.

By the time I heard the diesel's air horn, I could also hear the screaming brakes, but the engineer couldn't stop in time.

I swung around facing the train, and realized I had to jump. It was a hundred feet down to the icy river.

As I jumped, I saw a horizontal I-beam about eight feet below the rails. Instinctively, I jumped for it.

I made it; I still don't know how. I found myself standing on the beam, and I was still clutching my fishing rod!

The freight screeched past on the rain-slick rails. Then I climbed back up onto the track.

The engineer looked back after he stopped to see if I was OK. Then he went on, and I hurried off the trestle. I'll never walk a track again.

Wild Dog Encounter

By Michael W. Clifford, Ft. Dix, New Jersey

During bowhunting season, I was sitting under a blowdown tree alongside a fire lane. A doe ran up the lane, but I stayed where I was, hoping that a buck might have caught her scent and be following her through the woods.

In a few minutes, there was a noise in the woods. Thinking it was the buck, I got ready and waited.

Instead of a deer, a dozen wild dogs came out on the trail. They were following the doe's scent up the fire lane. But they picked up mine, and started toward me.

The dog closest to me started to growl and bare his teeth, so I let loose an arrow that went straight through and killed him.

My shot scared the other dogs off. Three or four ran down the fire lane and the rest went back down into the woods where they'd come from.

When the dogs ran away I thought they'd be scared off, and I started to relax. But they came back to get me. As fast as I could I shot the closest one.

The dogs stopped where they were. Close to panic, I yelled and ran at them. Finally they turned and ran off for good.

Ice Trap

By Joseph Small, Oak Lawn, Illinois

My friend Carl and I were pheasant hunting near Kankakee. Carl crossed the frozen Iroquois River on a down tree and I followed confidently because Carl had had no trouble.

I stepped off the tree on what I thought was solid ground and crashed right through.

I found myself in icy water above my waist but managed to crawl out on the real bank of the river. My legs were freezing.

At first, I couldn't figure out what had happened, but then I saw the hole I had made in the ice roof about six feet above the flowing water's surface.

I unloaded my gun, climbed the steep bank, and tossed it out. Then I squirmed through the hole. I was so cold I was stiffening up fast, and it was a struggle to get out.

I yelled for Carl, and he helped me to get home. We finally figured out that the river had frozen when the water was high, but then the water level fell, leaving the ice roof that I had taken for solid ground. Next time, I'll watch my step.

Hooked on Halibut

By Bill Lewis, Fairbanks, Alaska

My wife and I were putting out setlines for halibut off the coast of Alaska. I baited hooks while my wife maneuvered our boat.

The boat lurched and I stumbled into the line. Before I knew it, an unbaited hook had caught my sweater and was dragging me overboard.

The heavy anchor at the end of the line was pulling me deep. I tried to free the hook, but it had sunk in past the barb.

When my wife looked back and saw I was gone, she figured out what had happened and cut the boat's engines. She reversed the reel, hoping she had reacted quickly enough.

Gasping for air, I broke to the surface, with not a second to spare. My wife cut the line from my sweater and helped me back on board.

I was a little shaken but OK, thanks to my quick-thinking wife. I'll keep a close eye on those hooks next time.

Wrestling Match with a Deer

By Jim Babylon, Cedar Springs, Michigan

My son-in-law Rick and I were on a hunt for whitetails near a swamp in Michigan's Lower Peninsula. I shot a nice 7-point buck with my 16-gauge shotgun. He went down, apparently dead.

I put my gun on the ground and walked toward the buck. My shot had only stunned him and he suddenly got to his feet and lowered his antlers to gore me.

I grabbed his antlers to protect myself. Then I tried to wrestle him down the stream bank and into the water so I could drown him. At that point Rick ran up from behind me to find out what was happening.

Just then the deer broke free and began to run away. I grabbed Rick's 12-gauge shotgun and fired a shot.

The slug hit the deer and killed him. Rick and I were very careful when we walked up to that whitetail. I'll never approach another deer without my gun.

Close Call

By Billy Isom, Jacksonville, Alabama

Murphy Addison and I had just finished an elk hunt in the Colorado Rockies. We packed the meat in dry ice for the drive back to Alabama.

Late that night we decided to pull off the road and get some sleep in the camper.

About 45 minutes later I woke up unable to breathe. I could hear Murphy mumbling that something was wrong.

We barely had the strength to pull ourselves out of bed and on to the floor. We crawled to the door and pushed it open.

Out in the fresh air I thought my head would explode. Ten more minutes in that camper would have been sure death, I was told later.

From now on I'll never stay in closed quarters with dry ice. The carbon dioxide from "melting" dry ice displaces the air and drives the oxygen up and out making it easy to smother.

Dogged Courage

By Rob Roberts, Glenwood Springs, Colorado

Last spring my wife Laurie and I, together with Bo our Labrador retriever and Duchess, the family puppy, float-tripped the Colorado River.

We entered a stretch of whitewater and lost control of the boat when a high wave hit us. Capsizing, Duchess and I were thrown, but Laurie and Bo flipped with the boat.

The puppy and I were swept downstream and eventually washed ashore. We weren't hurt, but I saw that Laurie and Bo were trapped under the boat, which was caught broadside between some rocks. Minutes passed with no sign of them.

Bo suddenly broke water next to the boat. To my surprise, he dove down and disappeared under the boat.

Bo soon surfaced again—towing Laurie by her hair! Once clear of the boat, Laurie grabbed his tail as he swam ashore.

They both made it to safety with nothing more than a few minor scratches, thanks to Bo's devotion. The courageous Labrador went on to win the Ken-L Ration Dog Hero of 1982 award.

A Raging Boar

By William G. Guerne, Sebastopol, California

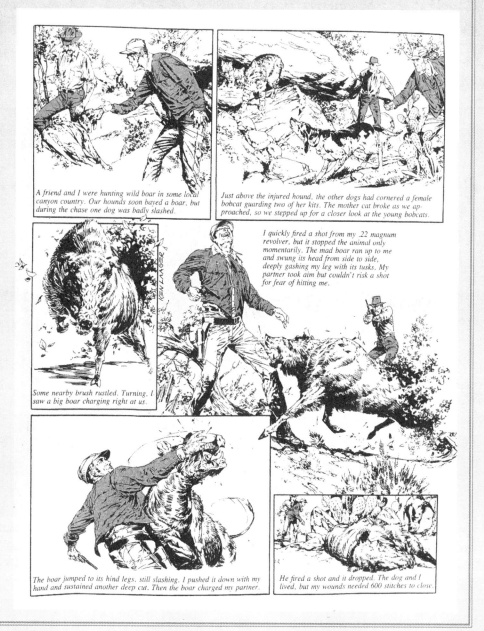

A friend and I were hunting wild boar in some local canyon country. Our hounds soon bayed a boar, but during the chase one dog was badly slashed.

Just above the injured hound, the other dogs had cornered a female bobcat guarding two of her kits. The mother cat broke as we approached, so we stepped up for a closer look at the young bobcats.

I quickly fired a shot from my .22 magnum revolver, but it stopped the animal only momentarily. The mad boar ran up to me and swung its head from side to side, deeply gashing my leg with its tusks. My partner took aim but couldn't risk a shot for fear of hitting me.

Some nearby brush rustled. Turning, I saw a big boar charging right at us.

The boar jumped to its hind legs, still slashing. I pushed it down with my hand and sustained another deep cut. Then the boar charged my partner.

He fired a shot and it dropped. The dog and I lived, but my wounds needed 600 stitches to close.

Hog Wild

By James B. Meade, Ruston, Louisiana

The thicket in north-central Louisiana was loaded with squirrels but the howl of my Bull Mastiff told me he had bayed something else.

My dogs were in a fierce battle with seven wild hogs. Two of my six dogs were severely injured and were bleeding.

I walked toward the commotion trying to call off the dogs, when a big boar saw me and charged. I quickly pumped three shots into his skull but he just kept coming, never hesitating.

The boar was on me in an instant. All I could do was fling my shotgun at him. I turned to run but fell and was at the hog's mercy. Sensing the danger, my dog grabbed the hog's tail.

The hogs crashed off into the brush. I reloaded my gun and took up the blood trail. I heard rustling behind me, spun and saw another hog on the charge. I stopped it in its tracks.

When my dogs heard the shots, they headed back toward me, barking. To be sure of no more surprise attacks, I climbed a nearby tree and waited until they arrived... without the hogs.

At the End of My Rope

By Larry E. Williams, Wilsonville, Oregon

Dawn broke on the Gulf of Mexico and, after an evening of spearing flounder, my brother and I grabbed our rods and began casting for redfish and speckled trout. We caught a number of fish, so I tied the heavily laden stringer to my waist and let it dangle in the water.

I spotted some larger gamefish attacking baitfish near a sandbar and felt we could swim across a channel and get into better casting position.

While swimming across the hole, a 10 or 12-foot blue-tipped shark grabbed the fish tied to my waist.

If the shark had swam the length of the channel I would have drowned. Instead, it headed across the sandbar, enabling me to struggle to my feet and call my brother for help.

My brother scrambled to my aid in an attempt to control the shark's run. Although it never came directly for me, the shark kept a firm grip on the stringer, trying to pull me along with it.

Finally, the tired shark loosened its hold on the stringer. Like a real fisherman, I had never let go of my fishing rod.

Hunting the Hunter

By Jim Snowdon, Vulcan, Michigan

I arrowed a nice spike buck late one afternoon last December. I took up the trail the next morning and quickly found the deer, but also spotted a dog stalking it nearby.

I decided to try and scare the dog off. It growled, stood its ground then slowly moved off.

About five minutes into the procedure, I suddenly felt something jump on my back, shoving me forward a few feet. The dog had returned.

Although shaken, I figured my ordeal was over and got back to the business at hand—gutting my downed buck.

I looked up to see the dog snarling and growling at me. I tried to fend it off, but the dog sunk its teeth into my flesh. Armed with my knife, I stabbed at the dog.

Finally, the dog let go of my arm and dropped over dead. I was bleeding badly. I managed to put the animal in my truck, then took it to the hospital where doctors stitched my wounds and later determined that the animal was not rabid.

Taken with Tuna

By Brad Moore, Five Islands, Maine

With the last day of the tuna season rapidly approaching, we pulled alongside a dragger and set lines, hoping that their chum slick would draw in fish.

We quickly hooked into a large tuna, hauled hard on the rope, and readied the harpoon. A second tuna hit but broke free. Although harpooned, the first fish was still alive.

We gave the fighting tuna more rope, hoping it would tire itself out. The tuna zoomed off, taking a tangle of hooks and lines with it. One hook sliced into my hand, sweeping me overboard.

Skipper Ken Pinkham reacted instantaneously. He grabbed the rope, dug his heels, and hauled back.

With adrenaline racing through his body, the skipper managed to horse in more than 700 pounds of man and fish. Inside a minute, we both flopped on the deck.

"Don't get out of the boat again," he shouted at me as he cut the hook protruding through my hand. Doctors later stitched my wounds.

Sabre-Toothed Bear

By James M. McCall, Tucker, Georgia

My dog Sabre and I were out hunting along a mountain trail in western Virginia when I heard four rifle shots crack the stillness of the autumn afternoon.

We continued walking toward the car when I spotted a black bear running over the hill and coming at me. The bear was growling and I could see it had been hit.

We ran for the car, Sabre diving through the window. I got in just as the bear arrived.

I attempted to crank up the window, but the bruin, its head half inside the car, tried to get at me. To my surprise, Sabre jumped over me, fighting and barking at the swiping bear. As the bear reached in again, Sabre bit into its paw.

I suddenly remembered that I had a .45 pistol on my hip. As I drew the gun, the bear suddenly slumped to the ground beside the car.

Three hunters, who had wounded the bear, arrived in minutes, apologizing for what had happened. My three minutes of terror seemed more like hours.

Thrown for a Loop

By The Rev. Gilbert B. Moore, Lander, Wyoming

The Wind River Mountains have been one of our favorite hunting areas for several years. My two sons, Jim and Dan, were hunting with their wives when they spotted a nice bull amid a harem of cows. Dan took careful aim and fired. The elk fled.

Thick foliage camouflaged the elk, which seemed to be waiting in the stream for Dan. The bull caught him by the belt loop on his trousers and tossed him through the air.

Dan tracked the bull, but lost the trail near a stream. There was no sign the elk had crossed, but Dan leaped over it.

Dan found himself in the stream, face to face with an enraged bull. Keeping an eye on the elk, he slowly moved toward the rifle he'd lost in the encounter.

Dan found his rifle before the elk charged again. He threw the gun to his shoulder and fired.

We all shudder to think what may have happened had the bull slipped a tine under Dan's leather belt instead of through the loop.

The Meanest Wolverine

By R. W. Enderlin, Alturas, California

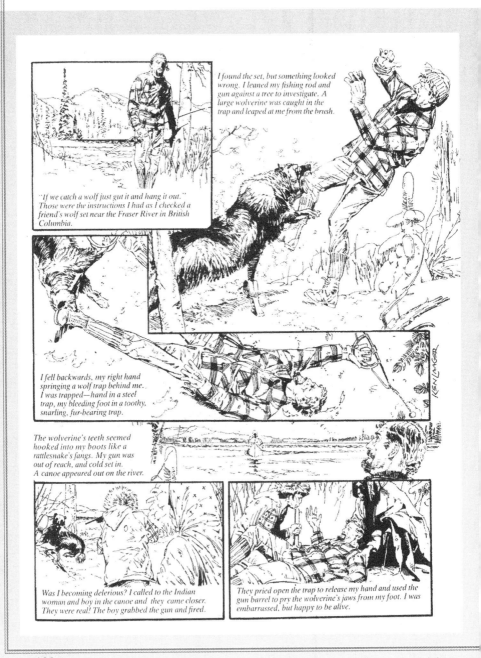

"If we catch a wolf just gut it and hang it out."
Those were the instructions I had as I checked a
friend's wolf set near the Fraser River in British
Columbia.

I found the set, but something looked
wrong. I leaned my fishing rod and
gun against a tree to investigate. A
large wolverine was caught in the
trap and leaped at me from the brush.

I fell backwards, my right hand
springing a wolf trap behind me..
I was trapped—hand in a steel
trap, my bleeding foot in a toothy,
snarling, fur-bearing trap.

The wolverine's teeth seemed
hooked into my boots like a
rattlesnake's fangs. My gun was
out of reach, and cold set in.
A canoe appeared out on the river.

Was I becoming delerious? I called to the Indian
woman and boy in the canoe and they came closer.
They were real! The boy grabbed the gun and fired.

They pried open the trap to release my hand and used the
gun barrel to pry the wolverine's jaws from my foot. I was
embarrassed, but happy to be alive.

A Wired Moose

By Game Warden David C. Priest, Maine

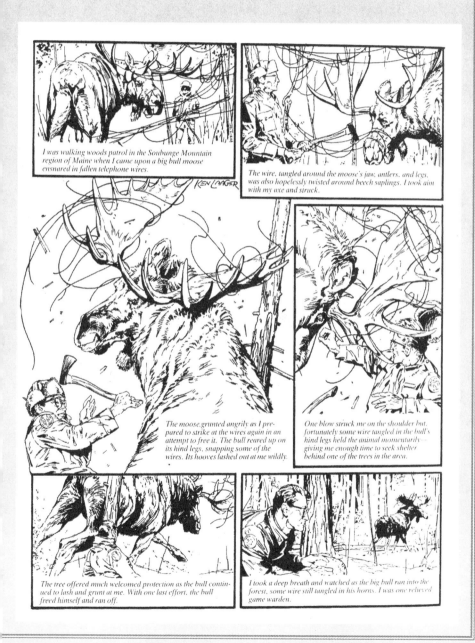

I was walking woods patrol in the Soubunge Mountain region of Maine when I came upon a big bull moose ensnared in fallen telephone wires.

The wire, tangled around the moose's jaw, antlers, and legs, was also hopelessly twisted around beech saplings. I took aim with my axe and struck.

The moose grunted angrily as I prepared to strike at the wires again in an attempt to free it. The bull reared up on its hind legs, snapping some of the wires. Its hooves lashed out at me wildly.

One blow struck me on the shoulder but, fortunately some wire tangled in the bull's hind legs held the animal momentarily— giving me enough time to seek shelter behind one of the trees in the area.

The tree offered much welcomed protection as the bull continued to lash and grunt at me. With one last effort, the bull freed himself and ran off.

I took a deep breath and watched as the big bull ran into the forest, some wire still tangled in his horns. I was one relieved game warden.

Raging Raccoon

By Norman Danieisen, Piscataway, New Jersey

It was a cool, cloudy April evening when I heard my dog, Sandy, barking outside. She was circling and barking at a raccoon.

Realizing that the coon was trying to drown Sandy, I jumped in and struck it with my flashlight.

Frightened, the coon jumped into the river, then turned on the dog.

Suddenly, the coon turned on me and bit into my left thumb. Its sharp teeth pierced both of my hands as I tried to pry its mouth open.

Knowing that raccoons can carry rabies, I had to kill it so that it could be examined. Drowning it seemed the only alternative.

A woodpile log left no doubt that the raccoon was dead. Luckily, the rabies test came up negative.

Hit and Run Bison

By National Park Service Report

Needing water, an Alaskan sheep hunter headed toward a nearby stream to fill his canteen. He heard rustling in the bushes.

Startled by the commotion, the hunter looked up to see a huge bull bison bearing down on him. It came so quickly that it was too late to move.

As if that wasn't enough, the hunter looked up again to see a grizzly coming at him.

The bison slammed into the hunter like a Mack truck, bending his backpack and leaving him dazed.

Fearing the worst, he scampered for his rifle and fired at the bear, grazing it slightly. The big grizzly stopped, turned and ran off into the woods.

Despite some serious injuries, the hunter survived. Just down the trail were other bison, one of which seemed to have been attacked by the bear.

Little Girl, Big Bear

By Jimmy Allen Craig, Fox Lake, Wisconsin

I was out bear hunting with my 9-year-old daughter, Lisa, when we spotted a sow with two cubs.

As I dove for the tree branch, the bear bit my leg. I smacked her in the nose.

The sow stood, then charged. My little girl ran for the safety of our nearby pickup truck as I ran for a tree to draw the sow's attention.

The sow pulled back, giving me time to climb higher. I looked down to see the pickup.

My little girl was at the wheel of the truck, yelling at the bear and beeping the horn to scare it away from the tree. Virtually undisturbed, the bear never yielded.

Lisa calmly grabbed hold of the 12-gauge shotgun in the truck, loaded it and shot at the bear. I climbed down and was later treated at the hospital. It took 26 stitches to close the gash in my leg.

Fox in the Foyer

By Bob Caldwell, Hasting, Ontario

My wife, son, and I had just finished eating lunch when I heard a noise outside. It was a large fox.

The fox set its sights on my dog, Gunner, a golden retriever. We watched from the window in horror as the drooling fox sank its teeth into Gunner's tail.

Gunner fought back valiantly, but the fox acted crazed. It screamed, jumped at the patio window, attempting to attack my wife, chewed the door, and bit into the screen window frames.

Inside, I searched in vain for gun ammunition. On the patio, the horrible fight continued. Gunner tried to escape through a screen window. The fox tore at another screen, trying to follow.

Finally, I found two .22 shorts. The fox was about to continue its attack when I slid the patio door open and fired.

Gunner stared quizzically, as if to ask if he had done the right thing. The fox, we later learned, was rabid. Although Gunner was vaccinated against rabies, he had to be destroyed due to his wounds.

Quicksand

By Marguerite Reiss, Anchorage, Alaska

It was a perfect day for duck hunting. Mike Spaulding and two buddies set out for the tidal flats outside of Anchorage.

Spaulding was about to retrieve a downed duck when the earth gave way. The more he tried to hurry the 85 feet to shore, the deeper he sank—quicksand.

Unable to free him, one of his buddies went for help. When firemen arrived, they extended a rope to him, and pulled.

Spaulding remained hopelessly mired, and with the tide quickly approaching, his fate seemed sealed. Attempts to dig him out were fruitless.

In a last ditch effort to free the victim, firemen crawled out on a ladder with a fire hose, hoping the jet stream would free his legs.

The incoming tide was just 30 minutes away when Spaulding took his life into his own hands. Grabbing the fire hose, he forced the nozzle into the top of his waders. The jet of water ballooned his hip boots just enough to free one leg, then the other. Medics kept close watch on him, once he was taken to the ambulance. Spaulding was treated for hypothermia and later hospitalized.

Mayday on Hammond Bay

By Harold DeHart, Onaway, Michigan, as told to Tom Huggler

The waves on Hammond Bay were three to five feet when buddy Harry Wheaton, his son Carl, and I decided to take a May run for lake trout. We were in about 40 feet of water.

Commercial fishermen work this area, so we tried to avoid their nets. Suddenly, I noticed a trap net marker.

Before I could change course, our cannonballs and lines became tangled in the net. We were held fast. Our propeller was also ensnared, and waves began pouring in.

We tried to reach someone on the CB radio, but to no avail. Suddenly, the boat capsized and tossed us into the 47° water of the bay.

Shore was too far away, so all we were able to do was cut the boat free and try to stay with it. A boy playing basketball on shore apparently saw everything that had happened.

The youngster ran to his beached dinghy, and with help from his seven-hp outboard, managed to motor out to rescue us from our life and death predicament.

Predatory Predicament

By Ed J. Bechaver, Manassa, Colorado

Last winter, my 16-year-old son, Brian, was leaning against a barbed-wire fence and blowing a predator call, when a large coyote trotted out 50 feet away.

After shooting the coyote and seeing it drop, Brian walked up to the seemingly dead animal.

Suddenly, the coyote sprang to its feet and leaped for Brian's throat. Brian tried to deflect the coyote with his rifle, but the coyote bit the gun's forend.

Brian managed to push the animal away as it splintered the forend; then he turned and ran when the coyote started to gnaw on the rifle's buttstock.

The coyote caught Brian by the calf within 100 feet, and they both went down. Brian tried to choke the animal, but to no avail. He was finally able to reach the knife on his belt and cut the coyote's throat.

Brian was treated and released for bites and cuts on his hands and his calf. An examination of the coyote showed no signs of rabies.

Bear in the Bedroom

By Rolland Hunt, as told to Daniel Hunt, Canyonville, Oregon

Awakened by a loud noise from my children's bedroom, I grabbed a flashlight to investigate. The screen above their bed was ripped open.

Apparently searching for food, a large black bear had climbed over the boys on its way to the kitchen.

The bear found a closet instead and began ripping its way through the wall. I ran for my rifle and returned to see the bear headed for my two boys.

I fired the .30/06 and hit the big bruin in the front shoulder. He dropped in a fit of rage and roared.

Fearing for the lives of my two sons, Rich and Wayne, I rushed over to dispatch the big bear. I placed a shot behind its ear, and the bear finally lay dead. It was a summer night not ever likely to be forgotten. A loud noise that I had thought was made by two mischievous boys turned out to be a bear.

Cabin Fever Bear

By R. W. Enderlin, Alturas, California

It was 2 a.m. in British Columbia. The dead silence was broken when our small shack trembled and shook.

I went to investigate. Cracking the door open, I saw a huge bear standing on its hind legs and popping its teeth. It seemed obvious to me that the bear was intent on coming in.

Almost without thinking, I grabbed a heavy cast-iron skillet that lay on the stove and swung. The bear deftly whacked it away.

I slammed the door closed in the bear's face and groped for my rifle. Just when I found it and worked a shell into the chamber, the bear smashed right through the door.

With no time to think, I thrust the barrel toward the bear, yanking the trigger just as the bear raked the leg of my long johns. Hit in the neck, the bear reeled back.

Roaring, the bear regained its feet and charged. This time, I finished it off. The next morning, my buddy Fred and I taped the bear and measured it at 8 feet 11 inches.

Iceberg!

By Doug Twichell, Dimondale, Michigan, as told to Tom Huggler

Rick Dunlap and I were fishing near the Cook nuclear plant on Lake Michigan for ice-out browns. There were numerous icebergs in the area.

A large iceberg moved too close for comfort and, before I could push our boat away, the berg had become entangled with the anchor rope. We were sinking.

Rick tossed me a fillet knife to cut the rope. I lunged but the knife stuck in the ice and my hand slipped along the blade, slicing open my palm.

Meanwhile, my partner and gear went into Lake Michigan. Our boat slipped from sight. I leaped to safety by clambering aboard the iceberg.

Foolishly, we had removed our life jackets earlier to use as cushions. Rick made his way toward me through the icy water and I managed to help him climb aboard.

We shouted for help and were inexplicably ignored by a nearby boat. Finally, another boat noticed our predicament and rescued us. My boat resurfaced, minus $300 worth of tackle. It took 17 stitches to mend my cut.

Devilfish!

By William E. Schaefer, Chula Vista, California

My three buddies Jose, Pablo and Jim were fishing near Costa Rica when they spotted a manta ray surfacing near their boat.

Jim headed to the front of the boat to raise the anchor in preparation to move. With the anchor half-raised, Jim cleated down to get a pair of gloves.

Below the surface of the water, the huge manta ray became entangled in the partially raised anchor and length of rope.

As Jim approached the cabin, the ray yanked the boat sharply in an attempt to free itself. Jim fell overboard.

Unconscious, Jim quickly began to sink below the surface. Pablo kicked off his shoes and jumped in after him as Jose tossed in a life ring.

Free of the manta, the boat was again maneuverable. Jose worked the boat into position as Pablo and Jim surfaced safely.

A Lion in Winter

By John D. Lusk, Albuquerque, New Mexico

I was visiting my grandparents in Colorado for Christmas, and eager to try out my new predator call, headed out into the nearby foothills.

I soon noticed movement, which I recognized as being a cougar. The cat closed the distance.

I grabbed my walking stick and stood up in hopes of scaring the cat off. The lion snarled and circled, looking for an opening.

Using my stick, I tried to ward the cougar off. It slapped the stick away and pounced.

I grabbed the lion around the neck in an effort to get it off me, but slipped in the snow. We both tumbled end over end down the slope.

We landed in a heap of flying snow against a tree. The lion shook itself, then slunk off down the canyon.

A Flying Gaffe

By Sharon Van Valin, Port Alsworth, Alaska

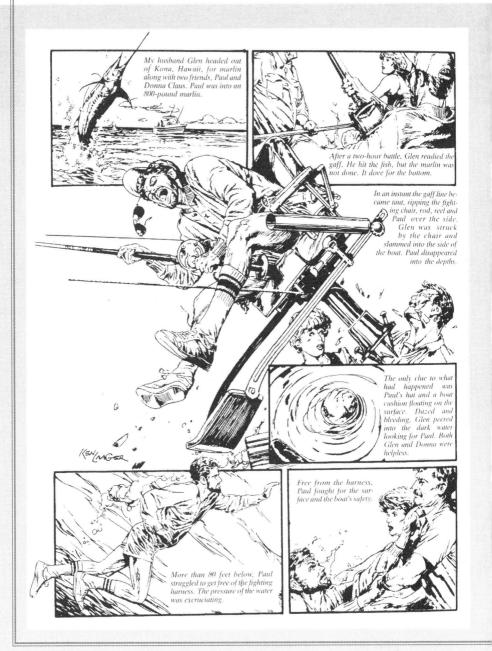

My husband Glen headed out of Kona, Hawaii, for marlin along with two friends, Paul and Donna Claus. Paul was into an 800-pound marlin.

After a two-hour battle, Glen readied the gaff. He hit the fish, but the marlin was not done. It dove for the bottom.

In an instant the gaff line became taut, ripping the fighting chair, rod, reel and Paul over the side. Glen was struck by the chair and slammed into the side of the boat. Paul disappeared into the depths.

The only clue to what had happened was Paul's hat and a boat cushion floating on the surface. Dazed and bleeding, Glen peered into the dark water looking for Paul. Both Glen and Donna were helpless.

More than 80 feet below, Paul struggled to get free of the fighting harness. The pressure of the water was excruciating.

Free from the harness, Paul fought for the surface and the boat's safety.

The Last Stand

By Daniel Ness, Erskine, Minnesota

It was opening day of Minnesota deer season, and I climbed into my favorite stand.

My wife and I were awaiting the birth of our second child, so I planned to hunt for just a few hours in the morning. The wind was blowing a gale and whipping the heavily falling snow with force. At about 7:15, I heard a loud crunch. I looked back to see a large poplar tree snap in a heavy gust.

Try as I might, I could not get out of the way. The tree was on me in an instant, knocking me completely out of my tree stand.

That's all I can remember. When I came to, I couldn't get my air. I managed to retrieve my rifle and fired several shots into the air, hoping that my brother, who was hunting nearby, would hear them.

Luckily, he did. When Todd found me, I was lying in the snow about 30 feet from the stand. With his help, we headed out to the truck.

We attempted to leave, but our truck bogged down in the snow. Todd pushed, and we got out. Surgery stopped the abdominal bleeding. Heidi Marie was born the next day, and I witnessed it all.

Moose by the Rafters

By Mike Bernard, Medford, Oregon

Three buddies and I were rafting down a river in Alaska when we spotted a cow moose and her calf attempting to cross the river ahead of us. We slowed the raft to give them a wide berth.

Suddenly, the calf lost its footing in the swift current. Despite nudges from its mother, the calf drifted downstream and drowned.

We pulled the raft ashore opposite the cow, but the moose began to move toward us. We scattered.

Apparently enraged, the cow moose charged us with her hackles raised. I lit out and headed for the nearest tree while my buddies headed up the bank in an effort to avoid the marauding moose coming after us.

After chasing my friends, the cow came after me. I quickly climbed a tree, but the moose circled it for more than two hours.

Finally, she gave up the attack and headed into the brush. We jumped into the raft and fled.

Rammed!

By Bob Oprondek, Champaign, Illinois

A colleague and I were selected by the University of Illinois for an on-foot tracking and movement study of sheep in the Sierra Nevada.

At about 10,000 feet, we were faced with a sheer, 35-foot rock face that we had to scale.

We reached the summit and before we had a chance to clear our heads, we were charged by two big rams.

The two full-grown rams were leading a group of 10 to 15 smaller sheep. Their brute force and lightning speed sent us plummeting to the canyon floor.

The fall took its toll. Dan's arm was broken. I had a broken thumb and numerous abrasions.

After a 20-hour march through 100° heat with very little water, we happened across two motocross riders who rescued us.

Hats Off to Rattlers

By George W. Suddarth, Lebanon, Tennessee

The deer were 175 yards out, feeding at the edge of the Alabama field, but it was obvious that both were nice bucks.

Afraid of risking an offhand shot at that distance, I decided that my only chance of taking a deer was to get down on all fours and crawl into better position.

I crawled head down in order to keep a low profile, and was almost in position when my cap was suddenly knocked from my head.

I reared up to see what had happened and saw a rattlesnake just in front of me, in a position to strike again.

Shaken and afraid of being bitten, I decided to act quickly. I chambered a load, shouldered my gun, and dispatched the big rattler.

I sat there for some time wondering why I hadn't heard the snake rattling. I then realized that the wind whipping the dry weeds had drowned out any noise that the snake might have made.

A Late Bill

By J.C. Zerby, M.D., Reading, Pennsylvania

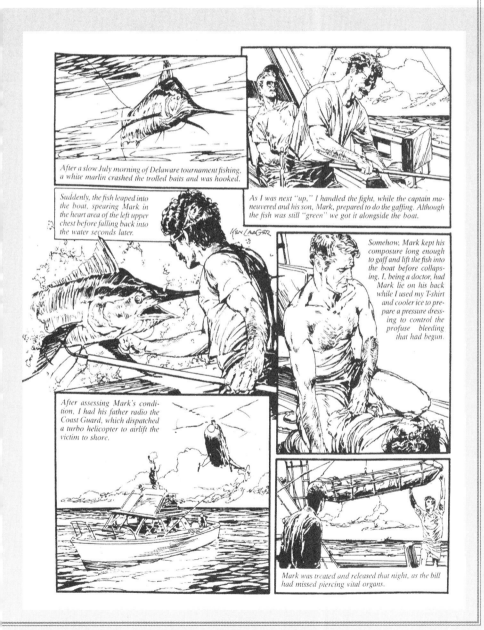

After a slow July morning of Delaware tournament fishing, a white marlin crashed the trolled baits and was hooked.

Suddenly, the fish leaped into the boat, spearing Mark in the heart area of the left upper chest before falling back into the water seconds later.

As I was next "up," I handled the fight, while the captain maneuvered and his son, Mark, prepared to do the gaffing. Although the fish was still "green" we got it alongside the boat.

Somehow, Mark kept his composure long enough to gaff and lift the fish into the boat before collapsing. I, being a doctor, had Mark lie on his back while I used my T-shirt and cooler ice to prepare a pressure dressing to control the profuse bleeding that had begun.

After assessing Mark's condition, I had his father radio the Coast Guard, which dispatched a turbo helicopter to airlift the victim to shore.

Mark was treated and released that night, as the bill had missed piercing vital organs.

Jumping the Gun

By William Alexander, Holmes, New York

Early in the deer season, my partner dropped me near my stand.

Just after the last swallow of coffee, I was surprised to see a nice buck standing no more than 50 yards away — an easy shot.

When I arrived, I knelt and placed my gun in its rack. Then I stepped back to line up the picture.

As the buck put its head down, I took aim with my new gun, felled the buck, and picked up my camera.

I was startled to see the buck get up. He quickly ran off with my new gun caught in his rack. Before I knew it, my deer and my gun were gone.

I could see that my sling had somehow been tangled in the buck's rack. The deer and my gun were never seen again, or at least there's been no report of them.

Leave It to Beaver

By Charles Mahaffey, Apache, Oklahoma

On a cold April day, I was fishing for crappies in an Oklahoma creek.

Soon I heard a beaver enter the water. I saw its bubble trail as it swam harmlessly past me, as other beavers had done over the years.

Suddenly, I was in pain and shock—the beaver had doubled back and torn into me.

Its teeth had sunk through my waders and coveralls. As I kicked at it to release its vise-like jaws, I lost a flipper.

Using one flipper, I struggled toward the shore and tried to hop up the steep embankment. The beaver did not attack again.

The puncture wounds on my upper leg appeared to be large. A doctor bandaged me and prescribed the rabies vaccine.

A Plane Drag

By J. D. Eberhardt, Renton, Washington

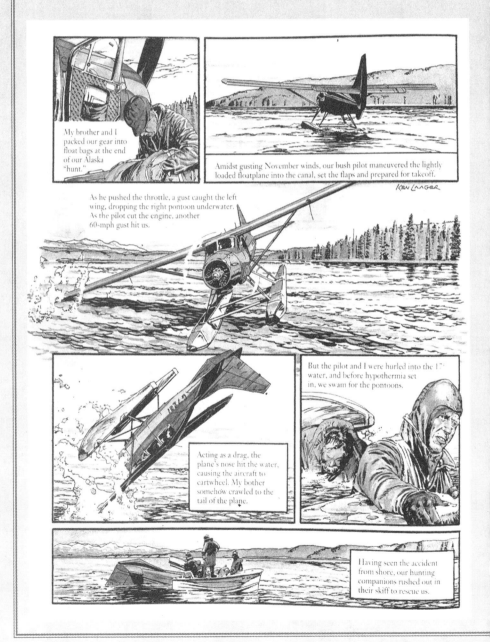

My brother and I packed our gear into float bags at the end of our Alaska "hunt."

Amidst gusting November winds, our bush pilot maneuvered the lightly loaded floatplane into the canal, set the flaps and prepared for takeoff.

KEN LAAGER

As he pushed the throttle, a gust caught the left wing, dropping the right pontoon underwater. As the pilot cut the engine, another 60-mph gust hit us.

But the pilot and I were hurled into the 17° water, and before hypothermia set in, we swam for the pontoons.

Acting as a drag, the plane's nose hit the water, causing the aircraft to cartwheel. My bother somehow crawled to the tail of the plane.

Having seen the accident from shore, our hunting companions rushed out in their skiff to rescue us.

Breaking the Bank

By Walter E. Sroka, Oneida, New York

Early one fall morning, I stopped to make a withdrawal at an automatic bank machine in Canastota, New York.

As I stood completing my transaction in the bank's glass-enclosed foyer, I was startled by a sudden loud crash.

A forkhorn buck had leapt through a plate glass window and was now stuck, half in the bank. The broken window had activated the bank's alarm system.

I freed the young forkhorn buck by gently pushing his head and forelimbs back through the shattered panel of glass.

The semi-conscious deer stood outside the bank, butting his tines against the glass, until he came out of his daze.

Apparently suffering no serious injury, the buck then made a quick getaway before the police arrived.

Log Jam

By Bailey Roberts, San Angelo, Texas

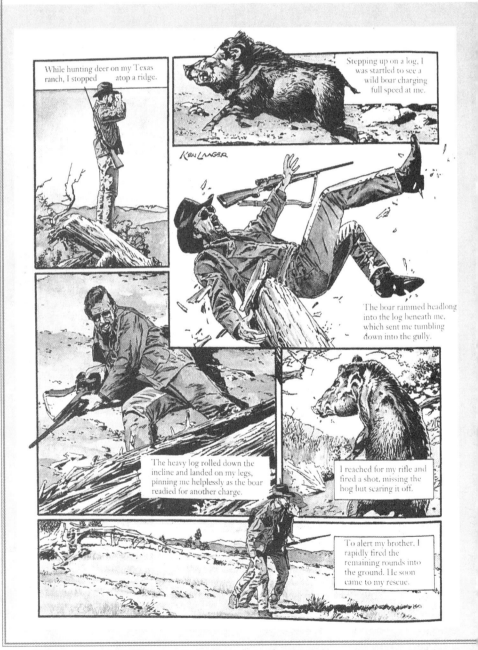

While hunting deer on my Texas ranch, I stopped atop a ridge.

Stepping up on a log, I was startled to see a wild boar charging full speed at me.

The boar rammed headlong into the log beneath me, which sent me tumbling down into the gully.

The heavy log rolled down the incline and landed on my legs, pinning me helplessly as the boar readied for another charge.

I reached for my rifle and fired a shot, missing the hog but scaring it off.

To alert my brother, I rapidly fired the remaining rounds into the ground. He soon came to my rescue.

Trapped!

By Michael J. Williams, East Poultney, Vermont

I was checking traps at a roadside culvert, where down a slope I had set a mink trap next to a deep pool.

Walking down the snow-covered slope, my feet slipped out from under me, and I plummeted into the water below.

I struggled in the icy water, but the weight of my gear and my water-filled waders pulled me under.

As I desperately reached out for some sapling branches on the pool bank, I felt something clamp down upon my fingers.

I had sprung my mink trap! Using the trap as an anchor, I was able to pull myself from the frigid water.

Other than bruised fingers, I had luckily escaped any serious injury.

Battle with a Badger

By James E. Crowley, Bennion, Utah

I was hunting deer last fall with my cousin.

Startled by a growl behind me, I turned to see a surly badger.

In an instant, the badger was just a few feet away. Fearing that the animal was rabid, I dropped my rifle and started running, calling to my cousin Tom.

Without being provoked, the animal suddenly reared up and charged. I shouldered my rifle and fired, but missed the fast-closing animal.

Tom heard my shouts and rushed to help. He sighted in on the badger and stopped it as it snapped at my heels.

We took the animal, which wasn't rabid, to a taxidermist, and it tipped the scales at 56 pounds. I never imagined a badger that big could move so fast!

A Rabid Attack

By Murray Rolph, Mill Iron, Montana

My family and I returned late from dinner one evening. I had entered the house with my wife, Rita, and three daughters when we heard a scream from our three-year-old son, Martin, still outside.

Rita rushed out and found Martin pinned to the ground by a large bobcat. The cat bit into the boy's neck and raked his stomach and legs with its sharp rear claws.

Rita jumped on the cat and freed Martin, but when she bent to lift the boy, the cat turned on her. It clawed her scalp, but couldn't reach her face.

In an attempt to ward off the attack, daughter Tanya beat the bobcat with the only weapon she could find—a phone book. It worked. Rita grabbed Martin and ran to the house.

Upon hearing the commotion, I ran outside, shotgun in hand. The ferocious bobcat attacked me from behind, hitting the gun barrel and biting my left hand.

I kicked the cat away and fired, killing it when it lunged for my throat. My wife and son needed stitches, and my whole family received precautionary rabies shots. Examination of the bobcat confirmed that it was rabid.

Snake's Alive

By W. Horace Carter, Hawthorne, Florida

My buddy Lindy Evans and I were fishing for bluegills when we spotted a snake near our boat. Lindy swatted at it with an oar and finally managed to ward it off.

Fish in hand, I opened the live well and was shocked to see the same snake wriggling around inside. It found the drain hole.

I slammed the lid shut but the snake, obviously a cottonmouth, was already halfway out. It was furious.

I grabbed a paddle to deter a strike but the big cottonmouth just sunk its fangs into it. Fearing a strike I jumped onto the console.

Unable to get at me, the snake made its way to the back of the boat. I kept trying to get a good poke at it but fishing tackle got in the way of my swings.

Finally, I found my opening and broke its neck with the paddle. I was lucky—a bite in 95° weather would have been fatal.

The Sting

By Dell Stephens, Richfield, Minnesota

My friend Bob, dog, Penny and myself headed out for a boat ride last summer. Our boat pounded the water as we crossed another boat's wake.

Bob suddenly noticed something coming from under the bow. Hornets—thousands of them —began swarming around us. Bob was stung.

He abandoned ship, losing his glasses in the process. The hornets turned their attention to me and Penny. I shut down the motor.

I jumped next and tried to coax Penny to follow. She snapped away at the angry swarm, then she, too, leaped over the side, bringing the hornets with her.

A man and his two children happened by and, seeing our plight, tried to help but were turned back by the swarm of hornets.

He retreated but returned after dropping off his children and rescued us. All of us had been badly stung but luckily did not need medical help. We returned that night to get the boat.

The Comeback

By H. Don Edson, Blair, Nebraska

2 I placed the mink on the floorboards to dry, poured a coffee and eased onto the dirt road to run the rest of my line.

1 A circuit of my trapline turned up a nice mink in one of the traps. I dispatched the large male with a spade and headed for my truck.

3 There was a sudden stirring in the darkened cab. I looked down at the floorboards and my eyes widened. The mink—very much alive—sprang at me! Coffee flew everywhere as the revived critter scrambled about to find an exit!

4 Flailing at the rocketing shadow, I wrestled the truck over to the shoulder.

5 I jumped out the door to escape the madness and the mink shot out behind me. He scampered into the woods where, as far as I was concerned, he deserved to live to a ripe old age.

A Blown Hunt

By Wade Thompson, Reston, Virginia

Just before daybreak, my concentration on the feeding scene below me was broken by an odd, intermittent sound of rushing air.

In a moment, the source of the noise appeared—an enormous hot air balloon ghosted over a ridge and was heading directly toward my ridgetop tree stand.

Apparently the balloonists were so busy capturing the scene on film they forgot about flying—the basket struck the top of my tree and spilled sideways, leaving the screaming occupants clutching for their lives 25 feet above me!

I was showered with branches while the pilot fired the flame. Frantic moments passed before the basket finally swung free.

Having witnessed everything from a distance, my hunting partner appeared under my stand and deadpanned: "Seen anything?"

Ice Breaker

By Bob Rosania, Phoenix, Arizona

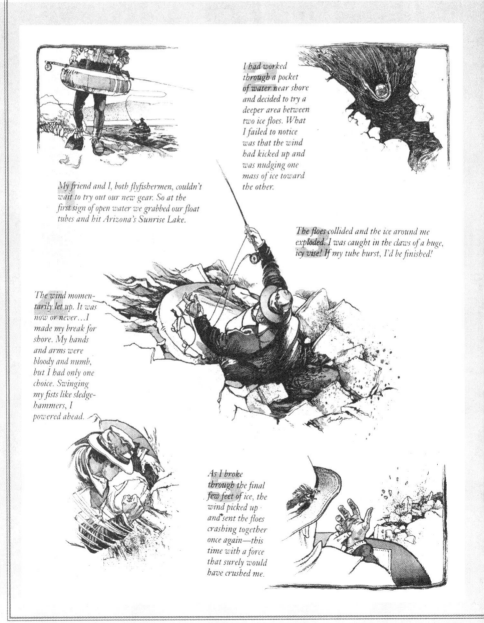

I had worked through a pocket of water near shore and decided to try a deeper area between two ice floes. What I failed to notice was that the wind had kicked up and was nudging one mass of ice toward the other.

My friend and I, both flyfishermen, couldn't wait to try out our new gear. So at the first sign of open water we grabbed our float tubes and hit Arizona's Sunrise Lake.

The floes collided and the ice around me exploded. I was caught in the claws of a huge, icy vise! If my tube burst, I'd be finished!

The wind momentarily let up. It was now or never...I made my break for shore. My hands and arms were bloody and numb, but I had only one choice. Swinging my fists like sledgehammers, I powered ahead.

As I broke through the final few feet of ice, the wind picked up and sent the floes crashing together once again—this time with a force that surely would have crushed me.

A Nutria Goes Nuts

By Ronnie D. Jinks, Winnsboro, Louisiana

I was relaxing in the soft glow of a quiet fishing evening when the sounds of a violent woodland brawl erupted behind me.

I turned to see a bobcat and a nutria, locked in each other's death grip, tumble down a steep bluff and into the water. Neither made it back to the surface, and calm slowly returned to the creek.

A few minutes later something thumped the bottom of my boat. The nutria was still alive...and he was mad as hell. The rodent clambered over the gunwale and came at me in a spitting rage. My Ruger .22—backup for cottonmouths—spit back.

I resumed fishing, although after that bizarre attack the remainder of the evening was anything but relaxing.